CHANNELING

CHANNELING
The Intuitive Connection

William H. Kautz, Sc.D.,
and Melanie Branon

Foreword and Forecast
by Kevin Ryerson

Harper & Row, Publishers, San Francisco

Cambridge, Hagerstown, New York, Philadelphia, Washington
London, Mexico City, São Paulo, Singapore, Sydney

To Phil,
for his objective feedback
and loving support

Library of Congress Cataloging-in-Publication Data
Kautz, William H.
   Channeling: the intuitive connection.
   Bibliography: p.
   1. Spiritualism. 2. Mediums. 3. Intuition
(Psychology) I. Branon, Melanie. II. Title.
BF1272.K37 1987   133.9   87-45181
ISBN 0-06-250451-7

87 88 89 90 91 HC 10 9 8 7 6 5 4 3 2 1

Contents

Foreword

What is channeling? How can channels help you? How can you integrate the information they give you into your lives, in both a practical and a spiritual way? How can you learn to be intuitive, perhaps even to channel?

In reading this book and searching for the answers to these questions, you are embarking on an exciting exploration into the world of intuition or "direct knowing." You will find that channeling is a not-so-mysterious way of tapping intuition, a natural faculty with which you were born.

Exploring channeling and the intuitive process is for the individual a journey of self-transformation. As you commit yourself to pursuing the intuitive path, over the days and years to come, you will find yourself gradually changing. You will no longer limit yourself to one particular method of rational, logical or empirical thought, but will eventually reach deeper into the richest source of information that you can possess—yourself.

But along your journey you will probably need some assistance. I certainly did during my own search for truth. That search began when I was an adolescent and became interested in such things as ESP, telepathy, and the afterlife. After several years of intense study and practice, my search culminated when I was about twenty-two years old and developed the channeling state. But it didn't end there.

About eight years ago, I met Dr. William Kautz, who was then working as a scientist at SRI International (formerly Stanford Research Institute) and independently conducting psychic research. He impressed me as a person who was both highly disciplined in science and highly sensitive to his own intuition.

One of the most knowledgeable entities, who speaks through me in the name of John, once said, "Science is the scribe that documents what God already knows."

Dr. Kautz took channeling and brought it into an entire new realm by showing how intuition can be a rich source of verifiable scientific information. He fulfilled a vision I always had of working in the context of futurism—harnessing intuition and logic to see what forces are shaping our society and how the future may bear out. He also became a mentor to me.

Dr. Kautz showed me how patient, diligent work with intuition can lead to the discovery and expression of one's deepest inner resources. He helped me harness and strengthen my own intuitive faculties. He respected me as a person with a unique talent, not outside the realm of possibility, that could benefit other individuals as well as society as a whole.

Now Dr. Kautz is once again sharing his extensive

knowledge about channeling and the intuitive process, this time with you.

Everyone who embarks on an exploration into a new area should do so from a well-informed position. In this book, Dr. Kautz and his co-author, Melanie Branon, give you a clear understanding of the channeling process so you can make intelligent decisions and exercise discernment while you explore. They show you how channels (such as myself) can intuitively guide individuals (such as you) along your personal journey to self-discovery.

While you are developing your own intuition, skilled channels can be a wonderful source of information and inspiration for you. Throughout this book, different channels (including yours truly) explain how they developed their intuitive skills and share the methods they use in working with people. Specific case histories—including excerpts from actual readings along with clients' comments—show you how channels have helped people solve problems, gain deeper insight into themselves, and improve their personal circumstances.

There is a classic metaphysical principle that matter follows thought. As you apply the insights about channeling and intuition that you gain from this book, your way of thinking, your perception of reality, will begin to change. As you progress along your own intuitive path, your individual growth will have an impact on others, first in your personal relationships and then in group dynamics. And as more and more people follow in your footsteps, that impact will multiply and branch out—until you all collectively participate in shifting the paradigm, or world view, this society currently holds. Then you will indeed become the "New Age" of consciousness that awaits you now.

I wish you the best of fortune in your intuitive exploration.

Kevin Ryerson

Acknowledgments

Through channeling, we have both discovered deeper dimensions to our own lives, as well as exciting possibilities for broader applications of this intuitive process. Through this book, we hope to share that enriching and inspiring experience with all of you.

Many thanks to the channels and clients who honestly and openly shared their often extremely personal experiences with us. A special thanks to Kevin Ryerson, not only for his channeled contributions, but also for his individual insight and warm encouragement.

For her constructive feedback and advice, our appreciation to Ruth Gottstein. For their editorial guidance and enthusiastic support, much gratitude to our editor, Tom Grady, and publicity director, Brian Erwin.

Most of all, profound thanks to our publisher, Clayton Carlson, for his timely vision and daring commitment.

Lastly, big thanks to little Trevor and baby Morgan, for letting their mother spend so much time on her " 'puter."

W.K. and M.B.

The names and identifying details of the persons mentioned in chapters 4 and 5 have been changed. The channeled information included is excerpted from actual readings.

1. Ancient Tool for Self-Awareness, or Metaphysical Magic Show?

> The most beautiful thing we can experience is the mysterious.
> It is the source of all true art and science.
>
> ALBERT EINSTEIN

Richard Lavin closes his eyes and fidgets in the hard aluminum chair, searching for a comfortable position. Bowing his head slightly, he breathes deeply. Suddenly, his shoulders heave up and his entire body shudders as though chilled by a gust of cold air. Then slowly, his shoulders settle down and he relaxes.

"Give us a moment, please," he murmurs and breathes again. His head rises, face calm and eyes still closed. "We are ready now," he proclaims.

Over the next two hours, a spiritual "entity"— someone or something named Ecton—will speak through Lavin's body in a mysterious process called "channeling."

What is this thing called "channeling?" The latest Hollywood breakthrough in special effects? A magician's triumphant slight of hand and eye?

Neither. Channeling is an age-old intuitive practice rapidly gaining popularity in modern Western society. Webster defines *intuition* as "comprehension without effort of reasoning" and *channeling* as "a means of access; a route." Put the definitions together, and *channeling* simply describes "a means of access to intuition."

Channeling is an inner process, an intuitive connection with a universal but unseen source of information and insight.

We hope this book will take the mystery out of channeling for you. The following chapters explain what channeling is and how it works. They describe how to distinguish good channels from bad, how to evaluate channeled information, and how to develop your own intuitive skills. Most importantly, they show you how channeling can put you on a personal path to self-discovery and fulfillment.

Our first goal, however, is to acquaint you with channeling. In this chapter, we will introduce you to channeling and different types of channels and then take you on a historical tour of channeling, from its ancient roots to the role it plays in your world today.

THE MANY FACES OF CHANNELING

Channeling is a mental process in which an individual, (the channel), partially or totally sets aside waking consciousness. Knowledge that lies beyond conscious awareness can then flow freely into the mind and be conveyed through speaking or writing to others.

How does all this internal activity appear on the surface? Channels vary widely in how they execute their intuitive skills, depending on which technique each uses to transcend the conscious mind. Some channels, called "sensitives" or "light-trance" channels, simply surpass the superficial aspects of the ego and tap into a higher state of consciousness, an impersonal reservoir of knowledge. No personality change is obvious; they converse normally or from a slightly meditative state.

Others, like Lavin, are called "deep-trance" channels because they appear to fall asleep while they enter an altered state of consciousness. Another personality or spiritual "entity" then emerges. These entities frequently possess distinct vocal qualities, mannerisms, and personal characteristics from their channels. Some claim to be nonphysical beings who have had prior lives on earth.

Take, for example, the entities "John" and "Tom McPherson," who communicate through channel Kevin Ryerson. John, who describes himself as an Essene scholar from the time of Christ, is believed by many to be a highly evolved entity. With a low, raspy voice, he delivers his messages in an Aramaic dialect. The loquacious McPherson speaks with the rolling brogue and irreverence of the Irish pickpocket he claims to have once been. Neither accent resembles the monotone of Ryerson's own delivery.

Similar differences were apparent when Jane Roberts (now deceased) channeled the entity "Seth." Seth spoke in a strong, male voice in contrast to Roberts's softer, feminine delivery. In addition, observers claim that Seth used gestures and facial expressions, as well as verbal inflections, entirely unlike the channel's own mannerisms.

These are only a few examples of trance channels and the entities who communicate through them. Hundreds, perhaps thousands, of channels are presently practicing their intuitive skills in large cities and small towns across America—as the country gives birth to a "New Age" of consciousness.

AN AGE-OLD SOURCE OF INSPIRATION

Channeling itself is not merely a current fad, a recent addition to our modern reservoir of talents. History teaches us that while its practitioners have been called everything from saints to sorcerers, the practice of intuitive skills is as old as civilization itself.

For centuries, Eastern religions have centered around the belief that true knowledge comes from within. Zen Buddhists, for instance, search for "the light" or for wisdom by mentally climbing a ladder to the highest point of spiritual awareness. They believe when minds reach that pinnacle, called *satori* (enlightenment), they can break through the limits of conceptual time and space, and tap into the universal source of all knowledge.[1]

The Eastern discipline of yoga has for years helped people develop deeper self-awareness. Those yogis who most adeptly master the mind also develop psychic powers called *siddhis,* which manifest in such supernormal abilities as levitation, bilocation, and clairvoyance.[2]

Christianity, since its beginning, has revered and rewarded paranormal occurrences, but it calls them *angels, voices, miracles,* and *divine revelations.* From walking on water to curing the sick, examples of miracles performed by the master teacher Jesus fill the Bible. And Joan of Arc, the daughter of a peasant farmer in an obscure village in fifteenth-century France, first heard an angel's voice in her father's garden when she was thirteen years old. The voice eventually directed her to lead the victorious rescue of France from England's seige. Although Joan was burned as a witch by her English captors, the Catholic Church canonized her a saint.[3]

But lest anyone think these psychic or revelatory powers are the private realm of mystical religious experiences, consider too the multitude of examples from the arts and sciences.

Artists, musicians, and writers have traditionally

tapped the unknown reaches of their minds for their inspirations, and have, in turn, been praised for their "creativity!" Brewster Ghiselin, in the *Creative Process,* reports that Max Ernst literally drew on his "powers of meditation" for visual inspiration. Henry Miller followed instinct and intuition for ideas to verbalize on paper. Wolfgang Amadeus Mozart fired up his "imagination"—where "in a pleasing lively dream" he would hear the parts of an ensemble not successively, but all at once![4]

Philosophers and psychologists have also struggled to unravel the mysteries of the mind and to discover the true source of inspiration and, indeed, knowledge itself.

In his book on Plato, R. M. Hare states that the father of philosophy believed that "the mind obtained knowledge of the eternal Ideas before it entered into the body at birth, and only had to recollect it in this life." Plato suggested that knowledge could then be found by looking into the soul for "the pure, the eternal, the immortal, the unchanging . . . wisdom."[5]

Swiss psychologist Carl Jung championed the concept of the unconscious mind as an invaluable source of knowledge and creativity. "Although the unconscious appears as a great shadow," he said, "it nevertheless contains unexpected light, inasmuch as it produces, among other things, illuminating inspirations." Jung claimed that artistic geniuses such as Shakespeare and Bach lived from their "creative depths," and he

described their works as "expressions of the unconscious unclouded by ego." He cautioned people that
if they did not nourish their instinct, their creativity
would "dry up."[6]

Ironically, science—the fortress of logic and reason—has felt perhaps the greatest impact of intuition.
Some scientific historians claim that virtually all great
scientific discoveries can be credited to intuitive insight rather than to deductive and inferential reasoning from "the facts." Einstein, for example, repeatedly
acknowledged the role of the intuitive leap in his discoveries, including the theory of relativity.

And Friedrich August von Kekulé, professor of
chemistry at Ghent in 1865, while dozing before his
fire dreamed of a snake seizing its own tail. He awoke
suddenly with the then-revolutionary idea that certain
organic compounds, such as benzene, are not open
structures of atoms, but form closed chains or
"rings."[7] Therein was born the basis for modern organic chemistry.

Other scientists credit intuitive associates, not
scientifically knowledgeable, for their advances. The
late J. Norman Emerson, a University of Toronto pro-
fessor and founder and president of the Canadian
Archaeological Association, worked with channel
George McMullen to identify a number of Native
American (Indian) artifacts and community sites in
Ontario. The sites were successfully excavated, and
McMullen's descriptions of their contents were

confirmed with a 80 percent rate of accuracy.[8]

These are only a few of the many examples of intuitive practice that have been handed down throughout the world's history.

SPIRITUAL STRUGGLE IN AMERICA

But if channeling has been practiced for centuries—by respected religions, artists, and scientists all over the world—why hasn't it been publicly acknowledged here in America?

Well, during the latter half of the 1880s, it was. For a while, at least. The first major metaphysical movement in America was instigated by the publication of *Nature's Divine Revelations* by Andrew Jackson Davis. The book, which posed the possibility of communicating with spirits, started America openly talking about and investigating spiritual sources of information.

By 1852, the words *trance-medium, seance,* and *clairvoyance* became casual terms of dinner conversation.[9] People claiming psychic powers vied for public attention. Some were believed genuine; others were proven frauds.

Daniel Douglas Home was the most famous and most credible medium of the time. Born in Scotland, Home moved at an early age to New England where he lived with his aunt. Home's unexplainable clairvoyant feats soon earned him a widespread reputation. He drew a great deal of attention from the nobility and literata of the day. Several people, including scientists, observed Home but could not provide any "normal" explanation for his abilities.[10]

Interest in mediums was thriving in England, too, which in turn further fueled the American movement. Sir William Barrett, a professor of physics, Edmund Gurney and F. W. H. Myers, academicians, and Henry Sidgewick, a philosopher, founded the Society for Psychical Research to explore psychic phenomona on the other side of the Atlantic.[11] In 1885, Barrett convinced American scholars to open a branch of the SPR here. Psychologist William James was one of its active members. By the late 1800s, mystic communications had filled the air in America.

But the early 1900s turned Americans' heads and hearts to survival issues brought on by war and depression, hardly environments fertile to inner exploration. And by the mid-1900s, the technological age was in full swing, entrenching Americans in "left-brain," analytical methods of research and discovery. Science reigned paramount. Investigation of inner sources of knowledge was put on the back burner.

In his book *Higher Creativity*, Willis Harman describes how a scientific taboo existed—and still exists—against inner knowledge:

Modern science developed in an industrializing society that put high value on those kinds of knowledge that would contribute to the generation of mechanical technologies.

This emphasis led to a tendency to test all knowledge by its usefulness in predicting and controlling the natural world.[12]

Consequently, orthodox science has since largely ignored the study of human consciousness, which cannot be so tangibly measured.

But science could not prevent individuals from searching for answers that it couldn't provide. And no skeptic could stop the spreading popularity of Edgar Cayce, the humanitarian psychic who dramatically changed the public perception of channeling in twentieth-century America.

In his conscious state, Cayce was a humble man with an eighth-grade education, who taught Sunday School. But while in self-imposed hypnotic trances, Cayce delivered incredibly detailed medical diagnoses and profound philosophical dissertations. At all times he held the highest of ethical standards; he used his psychic skills only to help humanity.

In 1910, the *New York Times* ran a two-page story about Cayce's clairvoyant successes in healing. From then on, sick or troubled people from all over the country, sometimes other parts of the world, sought psychic advice from the "Sleeping Prophet."[13]

Cayce's more than 14,000 "readings" encompassed mostly medical issues but also covered philosophical topics ranging from creation to reincarnation. As his medical diagnoses became reknowned for their

incredible scope and accuracy, his noble work raised
the credibility of channeling to new heights. And his
philosophical dissertations touched a responsive chord
in the masses who believed in the metaphysical truths
he proclaimed.

Even the advent of high technology and all its
promises of electronic life improvements didn't dimin-
ish Americans' search for a deeper meaning in their
modern existence. In fact, it only stoked the fire beginning to burn beneath society's surface.

Slowly, an underground movement swelled until a
silent earthquake split the country into two sides. In
Megatrends, John Naisbitt aptly calls this cultural chasm
"high tech/high touch." For while many Americans
were enthralled with high technology's new tools and
toys, others were dismayed by the country's loss of
personalism and humane values.

Naisbitt writes:

Our response to the high tech all around us was the evolution of a highly personal value system to compensate for the
impersonal nature of technology. The result was the new
self-help or personal growth movement, which eventually
became the human potential movement.[14]

The human potential movement of the 1960s gave
birth to various forms of spiritual exploration such as
Erhart Seminar Training (est), transcendental meditation (TM), Rolfing, and yoga. And it stimulated a

still-thriving interest in Eastern religions such as Zen Buddhism, which has secured a strong foothold in the West.

Although each of these disciplines offered its own approach for expanding consciousness, all had the same goal: to reach "enlightenment"—that heightened state of awareness where ego disappears and the mind is reconnected with the divine dimension of the universe, the source of all knowledge. In that intuitive state, says John White in *New Realities,* "all the long-sought answers to life's basic questions are given, along with peace of mind and heart."[15]

A NEW AGE DAWNS

Since the tumultuous 1960s, when the seeds of spiritual transformation were planted in America, all may appear to have been quiet on the Western front. But it has not been inactive. The New Age movement has established roots and is starting to grow. More and more Americans are taking a holistic approach to contemporary existence. They are recognizing the integral role the mind plays in determining destiny. And they are claiming personal responsibility for their diet and health, their living and dying.

And while the movement is still primarily underground, its effects are beginning to surface in all aspects of today's society. Hypnosis, once considered the realm of the theater, is now recognized and respected as a valuable therapeutic technique. Biofeedback is being used in lieu of drugs to relax the muscle tension that causes headaches, to control pain, and to change brain wave patterns. Holistic health centers and hospices, offering various combinations of new healing techniques and traditional medical treatments, are sprouting up all over the country.

People everywhere are eagerly exploring the powers of the mind. And they are transforming a previously meager subculture into a thriving consumer market for metaphysical information.

Major bookstore chains are stocking "mainstream" books on subjects like "lucid dreaming," "intuition," and "subliminal persuasion," topics previously hidden in the occult racks or carried by specialty shops.

Corporate executives are jumping on the bandwagon by enrolling in creativity classes and learning how to use intuition in management.

And increasing numbers of people everywhere are asking professional channels or themselves, "What is my purpose in life?"

This massive movement of inquiring minds is growing rapidly and cutting across all economic and social stratas. In *The Aquarian Conspiracy,* Marilyn Ferguson describes the movement's members:

The Aquarian Conspirators range across all levels of income and education, from the humblest to the highest. They are schoolteachers and office workers, famous scientists, government officials and lawmakers, artists and millionaires, taxi drivers and celebrities, leaders in medicine, education, law, psychology.[16]

But while some are willing to speak openly about their metaphysical interests, others prefer to stay underground, says Ferguson, "believing they can be more effective if they are not identified with ideas that have all too often been misunderstood."

All too often misunderstood, indeed. Therein lies the key to the American public's resistance in the past to intuitive techniques like channeling.

THE LAST OBSTACLE: OVERCOMING FEAR

Most people tend to fear things they don't understand. Why else was Jesus crucified, Socrates poisoned, Columbus scorned, and Joan of Arc burned?

And the American public, in particular, has learned from the country's influential media to be afraid of anything that smacks of the "supernatural"— including channeling. The media, especially movies, have in the past portrayed "psychic powers" only in the terrifying terms of evil possession.

Who could remain unfrightened after watching young Regan's possessed head turn around and around on her shoulders as she screamed obsenities in *The Exorcist?*

Who could not bemoan the cruel psychic fate of

poor Johnny Smith, the car-crash victim in Stephen King's *The Dead Zone.* When Johnny regained consciousness, his "extraordinary psychic powers propelled him into horror-filled, supernatural experiences" from which he desperately sought seclusion.

But while Hollywood today is still producing sensational misinterpretations of the "supernatural," it is beginning to pay homage to the New Age with some more recent—and more insightful—interpretations of spirituality on the silver screen.

Movies like *ET* and *Cocoon,* while whimsically scratching the spiritual surface, portrayed extraterrestrials in positive ways. Several of the *Twilight Zone* television shows sensitively depicted metaphysical subjects, such as reincarnation, time travel, and psychic power.

And *Out on a Limb,* the television miniseries based on Shirley MacLaine's bestseller of the same name, will probably go on record as having drawn more public attention to "raising consciousness" in the 1980s than TM did in the 1960s.

In *Out on a Limb,* MacLaine portrayed her "intimate journey inward" in which she was exposed—predominantly through channel Kevin Ryerson—"to dimensions of time and space that heretofore belonged to science fiction."[17] MacLaine's sensitivity, honesty, and sense of humor in confronting her inner self and the spiritual domain have inspired even the most skeptical observers. The discoveries she shared have served as a primer in metaphysics for millions. And Ryerson's "live" channeling during the televised movie publicly demonstrated what a powerful vehicle channeling can be for increasing spiritual awareness.

As the future unfolds and more and more people understand the intuitive process, channeling's contribution will be increasingly appreciated. Read on and discover how channeling can help you explore new vistas of understanding and find your private path to self-discovery.

2. Connections to Higher Dimensions

Man found that he was faced with the acceptance of 'spiritual' forces, that is to say such forces as cannot be apprehended by the senses, particularly not by sight, and yet having undoubted, even extremely strong, effects.

SIGMUND FREUD

Deep-trance channel Jon Fox, through whom the entity Hilarion communicates, describes what channeling feels like for him:

As I go into trance, a warm sensation flows from my lower back up through my spine. Sound changes frequency and I feel a slight pressure inside my head. As Hilarion enters, I clearly sense an altered space. When the transition is complete, I become less aware of any sensations.

And light-trance channel Penney Peirce says,

When I enter an intuitive state, I diffuse my personality. I become softer and softer until I become very large. In that largeness I have access to a wealth of fine information that somehow conveys itself back through my memory patterns to my conscious mind—where I'm ready to grasp it with words and describe it.

The broad scope and uncanny accuracy of the best channeled information have intensified public interest in the mysterious ways such knowledge is obtained. How do channels make this intuitive connection to a higher dimension, which offers them contact with disembodied spirits and access to a universal reservoir of apparently limitless knowledge? Or put more simply, how and where are channels getting their information?

THE INVESTIGATION OF INTUITIVE KNOWLEDGE

To date, there is no significant scientific understanding of the physiology or even the psychology of channeling; that is, of exactly what takes place inside the mind during channeling.

As we have seen, science has often placed such emphasis on logical and analytic methods of deduction that more intuitive sources of knowledge have been ignored. In *Awakening Intuition,* Frances Vaughan explains that while intuition plays a vital role in creativity, problem solving, and interpersonal relationships, it is often discounted as a reliable source of information. "Many people are frightened by experiences which seem unusual, illogical, or paranormal," she writes. So they choose to ignore what they don't understand. "But popular interest in the development of mental powers is prompting people to pay more attention to intuition," she notes.[1] New methods of studying and developing the neglected intuitive faculties are now being explored.

Vaughan reports that current mind-brain research metaphorically divides mental activity between the two hemispheres of the brain. The left hemisphere is believed to be responsible predominantly for rational, analytical thinking and most language. The right primarily provides the intuitive, esthetic, and pattern-related components of thought.

In order to increase creativity, which requires the balanced use of both halves, many contemporary thinkers and teachers are pioneering a greater emphasis on previously neglected right-brain activity. For example, Ned Herrmann, a New York management consultant, has developed a test to determine right-brain or left-brain dominance. He now teaches creativity seminars where participants learn to further develop the usually neglected right brain, where intuition occurs, and then apply both components in a "whole-brain" approach.[2]

There is also increasing scientific support for the mind's incredible potential when in an altered state of consciousness. Willis Harman, president of the Institute of Noetic Sciences, notes ironically that "although mystics, in one guise or another, have been telling people how to achieve this state for thousands of years, science has only officially begun to recognize it since it became possible to reproduce the experience under laboratory conditions, via biofeedback, where it could be quantified and analyzed."[3]

Using EEG (electroencephalograph) machines to register the rhythms of the brain, he says, scientists can now detect a "relationship between certain rhythms detected in the electrical activity of the brains of yogis and mystics when they have reached the deepest part of their meditations, and the stimulation of *higher* or *altered* or *mystical* or *unitary* states of consciousness."[4]

The results of recent scientific research, combined with the experiential studies of channeling conducted at the Center for Applied Intuition, have contributed to a better understanding of channeling and intuition. From that understanding, still in the embryonic stage, a simple "working model" of the mind has been created to help identify what conditions are necessary for channeling to take place.

A MODEL OF THE MIND

The working model, illustrated in this figure of concentric circles, divides the human mind into three parts.

THE CONSCIOUS MIND

First, the circle's core represents the individual *conscious* mind. It reflects the portion of total reality of which you are consciously aware: the largely physical world you experience through your senses. It includes

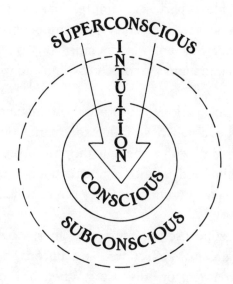

the rational and perceptual thought processes that transpire in your brain.

This is the part of the mind you normally use in daily activities. It doesn't have much memory and what little it has is short-term only. It simply has the ability to focus attention. For example, if you review your thought processes during a given day, you'll find that you're mostly shifting your attention from one thing to another.

THE SUBCONSCIOUS MIND

Surrounding this conscious core is the *subconscious* mind, a storehouse of memories. Throughout your life, you file experiences, impressions, and feelings here. If you want to remember something or someone, you deliberately pull the memory out of the subconscious mind into the conscious mind and work with it.

The subconscious also stores those incomplete experiences you may have found too fearful or uncomfortable to deal with at the time they first arose, usually during childhood. These fragments can be the source of much pain and suffering. They can continually limit you.

The subconscious surfaces most commonly through dreams, reflections, and unconscious reactions such as fear or "dis-ease." When you're awake, the subconscious is usually running the show. You act—or react—to stay in alignment with decisions you made previously and filed in your subconscious. However, subconscious material can be brought to consciousness and successfully confronted through meditation, prayer, hypnosis, and various other altered states of consciousness, properly induced.

THE SUPERCONSCIOUS MIND

Beyond the conscious and subconscious minds lies the expansive *superconscious* mind, an unlimited reservoir of knowledge transcending time and space.

In order to gain access to the superconscious, the conscious mind must transcend—or literally "channel through"—the subconscious. Then superconscious information can flow into consciousness. Everyone experiences this process occasionally, although there is usually considerable interference and distortion. With proper training, detailed later in this book, any conscious mind can learn to repeatedly reach the level of superconsciousness. There it can freely and clearly tap the kind of knowledge that might otherwise be accessible only through the enlightened state enjoyed by select yogis, Buddhists, and mystics.

The most important feature of the individual superconscious is its apparent universality. In contrast to subconscious memories, superconscious knowledge appears to be shared to a large extent (if not totally) with all minds. Herein lies *the record of all human knowledge and experience, past and future, actual and potential.*

This superconscious reservoir is similar to what Carl Jung called the "collective unconscious."[5] From the time he was a young boy, Jung personally experienced visions that could not be explained through his own memories. Some of these visions were precognitive; Jung found parallels in religious events that occurred many years later.

Jung divided the "unconscious" into two realms. The first, which our model calls the subconscious, contained personally experienced but forgotten or repressed contents. The second, comparable to the superconscious in our model, consisted of the "collective unconscious," an innate psychic structure encompassing the universal thought forms of all humanity from the beginning of time.[6]

Indeed, the major religions and cultures of the

world have long acknowledged the concept of the superconscious or a collective unconscious. They have bestowed various titles on it, including the "Akashic Records," the "Great Book," or the "Book of God's Remembrance." The Edgar Cayce readings most frequently identify the collective unconscious as the "Akashic Records," a name derived from the Sanskrit word *akasha* and referring to "the fundamental etheric substance of the universe, electrospiritual in composition."[7] These records, bearing every soul's thoughts and activities, can be read by channels who are able to attain a sufficiently ego-free state of altered consciousness, or by entities who have merged with channels' minds at the superconscious level.

TAPPING THE SUPERCONSCIOUS MIND

Channels have learned to quiet their conscious and subconscious minds so that superconscious knowledge can flow through them to consciousness in a graceful and communicable way. They tap directly into the superconscious reservoir of universal knowledge and relay the information they obtain there.

Channels use two basic methods to alter their consciousness and contact the superconscious: light trance and deep trance. Neither method is necessarily "better" than the other and each offers a unique perspective.

Light-trance channels partially set aside their normal consciousness through what looks like light meditation. But deep-trance channels completely set aside their waking consciousness and appear to fall asleep. Mentally, they may merge at the superconscious level with spiritual entities who convey information through them. In these cases, the channels' conscious minds may leave their bodies temporarily to be taken over by other beings who make use of their vocal cords. They are not, however, victims of "possession." These channels willingly allow entities to communicate through their bodies.

For some people, believing in nonphysical entities from higher dimensions is the hardest aspect of channeling to accept. Like angels or miracles, invisible sources of information require that you have faith; they ask you to believe in their existence without giving you tangible proof. For others, that same intangibility holds great appeal. The very possibility of communicating with spiritual beings—who have seemingly limitless access to information about the world and each individual in it—gives them hope and inspiration. But both skeptical observers and confirmed believers alike are eager to learn more about the origin of nonphysical entities.

TEACHERS OF THE UNIVERSE

What is a "discarnate entity"? Is it a disembodied spirit? An angel or some other representative of

"God"? A higher level of the channel's own conscious mind, which chooses to personalize itself in order to be more acceptable to listeners? No one knows exactly. The various personalities or entities who appear during channeling sessions describe themselves in all these ways. But although their biographies may vary, the majority profess dedication to the same purpose: guiding the spiritual growth of people on earth today.

For example, here is how Mentor, as channeled through Meredith Lady Young, explains these entities:

We are within—as part of your own evolving energy—and without—as a separate energy existing in a separate reality. We are of another more highly evolved plane with beings of greater understanding. We wish to augment your development through the teachings of cosmic truths. We wish you only the peace and joy of dynamic self-realization.

We and others of the universe have consistently interacted with your planet, Earth, and many other stars of your galaxy. It is universally understood that more highly evolved energies will be allowed to periodically transcend their energy bounds in order to share insights with more slowly evolving energies.[8]

The entity Michael describes his colleagues as "reintegrated fragments of a causal body no longer alive as you know it," who come to all who seek them. Their purpose is to teach "evolution on the physical plane so that the student can reach some insight into human behavior." He notes, "If one is to seek the path to spiritual enlightenment one must first become aware of one's own inner humanness, and exploit this to its fullest."9

Kevin Ryerson believes that the entities he channels do help people gain a higher understanding of the human condition. "These spirits have a broader perspective because they are not limited to the physical senses," he says. "And while they don't know everything, they are closer to truth and knowingness."

Whatever method a particular channel uses to tap into the superconscious reservoir of knowledge is not of utmost importance. What matters most is that the information you acquire from a qualified channel shines light on your spiritual path. In the next chapter, we will look at how intuitive information can help you understand your unique and perfect role in the all-encompassing, timeless picture of the universe.

3. A Holistic Approach to a Happier Life

All are but parts of one stupendous whole, whose body Nature is, and God the soul.

ALEXANDER POPE

A caterpillar crawling on the ground views only a small and limited part of the world. But when that caterpillar turns into a butterfly and flies up into the air, its perspective changes considerably. From even a few feet overhead, things that once appeared large and separate blend together like little pieces in a gigantic puzzle.

Many people, too, view individual problems or situations in their lives as separate issues to be addressed. They struggle with the why's and wherefore's of each circumstance, failing to understand how each event in life fits into a bigger picture.

Some allow their feelings alone to dictate their decisions. They live day to day in a whirlwind of emotional existence, driven by subconscious desires or fears.

Others seek purely intellectual solutions, believing that only logic holds the answers—until they realize that the intellectual route, too, can only be partially effective.

Finally, often in frustration or through crisis, these people add the spiritual component to their search for the truth. And they join the millions of people today who are seeking more holistic solutions to their problems.

These seekers are trying to balance the mental, emotional, and spiritual sides of themselves. They're trying to find meaningful links between outer and inner experiences. They're yearning for a deeper understanding of their true purpose in life.

STARTING YOUR SPIRITUAL JOURNEY

Embarking on any new journey can be a source of apprehension as well as excitement. So frequently novice seekers initiate their spiritual journeys by participating in a group observation of channeling, sponsored by a metaphysical or spiritual organization. The supportive atmosphere of similar inquiring minds grants them a comfortable—and often inspiring—introduction to channeling.

Several discarnate entities, who as teachers express great concern with human affairs on a grand scale, compassionately advise such groups about spiritual growth. Through their deep-trance channels, they tell listeners how to become more aware, more self-responsible, and more open to the truths that lie within them. And, perhaps most importantly, they help spiritual students appreciate their own power to create and influence the events in their lives.

But while group observation of channeling is a valuable means of increasing spiritual awareness, many people want more individualized counsel. So they seek private "life readings" from channels. (Other types of intuitive consultation are defined on page 81.)

Because channels access higher spiritual dimensions, they—or the entities communicating through them—can view or "read" each client's life from a broad perspective, seemingly undaunted by the limitations of time and space and unclouded by the client's intellectual constraints, confused emotions, or unconscious beliefs.

Moving amid the physical, mental, and spiritual aspects of a client's life, skilled channels are able to clarify issues concerning life purpose, career, relationships, health, and personal growth. Like spiritual butterflies, they can travel over the past, present, and future, gathering and assembling the missing pieces of the puzzle until they fit into one holistic picture.

Chapters 4 and 5, each a true account of an individual's experience with intuitive counsel, demonstrate how channels guide people along the road to greater self-understanding. But before you can truly appreciate these vignettes, you need to understand more about the metaphysical perspective of life.

LIFE: A QUEST FOR UNDERSTANDING

The question of what "life" is has puzzled philosophers, theologians, scientists, artists, writers, and spiritual seekers for centuries. It has evoked a myriad of metaphorical explanations and has been called everything from a "dream" to a "vast ocean of consciousness" to a "ungraspable phantom."

The entity Hilarion explains "life" through channel Maurice Cooke:

The real life is not at the physical level, but at the level of spirit.... All of material manifestation—every physical body, every plant, tree, sun, or planet of the cosmos—is merely a vehicle for learning, an article of clothing that is put on for a time, and then discarded. But the being that goes through this experience of taking up and setting aside is spiritual, and you yourself are one of these spiritual beings.[1]

As a spiritual being, explains Hilarion, you have come into bodies in order to learn about yourself so you can pass on to other levels. Complete self-understanding, he says, is the ultimate goal. But self-understanding cannot be achieved in a single lifetime. This should not come as a surprise, notes the entity Mentor:

Considering the slow progress toward awareness, and the fact that most people do indeed die short of enlightenment, it becomes obvious that to achieve even relative cosmic understanding, the soul body needs more than a mere eighty years on earth. It needs the constant course correction of birth, life, death and rebirth to begin to grow in understanding.[2]

And thus "reincarnation into the earth school" is necessary for the soul to reach its ultimate goal of self-understanding.

REINCARNATION: WHEEL OF REBIRTH

Reincarnation has been defined as "a rebirth in a new embodiment; the belief that souls are reborn." It holds that *you* are responsible for your own destiny. Decisions you make and actions you perform in one life directly affect others according to karma, the cosmic law of cause and effect.

William James said, "We are spinning our own fates, good or evil, and never to be undone. Every smallest stroke of virtue or of vice leaves its never so little scar." And Jesus Christ declared, "Whatsoever a man soweth, that shall he also reap."

Between lives, believe reincarnationists, each soul assimilates past experiences and assesses future opportunities—often with the help of other discarnate entities. This discarnate period offers the soul greater perspective but less opportunity for growth. So it chooses to manifest again in a new body and life situation.

Once a soul has incarnated, the door to the past temporarily closes so the individual can focus on the life at hand. But that door can be opened if an inquiring mind desires a deeper understanding of his or her origins.

THE LONG VOYAGE FROM EAST TO WEST

Reincarnation is not a new or unfamiliar theory to most of the civilized world, especially in the East. The two great Eastern religions, Buddhism and Hinduism, have always avowed that each soul progresses through many successive lifetimes. And ancient belief in reincarnation was not geographically limited to Japan, China, India, and Southeast Asia. History shows various populations of Africa, Australia, Central and South America to have been reincarnationists.[3]

But in the Western world, reincarnation today largely represents an alien concept. One reason for the estrangement is that reincarnation has not been proven scientifically to be a "fact." And in this technology-based and fact-driven society, some people need that assurance. They object "rationally" that if they had been here before they would remember previous lives. (Reincarnationists remind them that most people remember little of their early childhood—although it significantly influenced who they are today—without such psychological assistance as hypnosis.) Another reason is that in the West most of the population practices Judeo-Christian religions, which do not teach multiple and cyclic reincarnation. So the Eastern concept of reincarnation appears fantastic to them, says philosopher C. J. Ducasse, "because it diverges from the ideas of life and death to which they have been habituated from childhood."[4]

But ironically, and unrecognized by most of today's Christians, their religious ancestors widely believed in reincarnation. Indeed, the belief in reincarnation had a profound impact on religion and philosophy throughout the history of early Christianity, and in medieval and Renaissance Europe.

During Christianity's fledgling days, many different creeds existed, including those of the Christian Gnostics, who firmly believed in reincarnation. But the Council of Nicaea decided in A.D. 325 that reincarnation represented heresy and dropped it from the Bible, forcing the Christian Gnostics out of the Church. And the Emperor Justinian held an unofficial Fifth Ecumenical Council in A.D. 553, during which he issued "anathemas" against the doctrine of "pre-existence of the soul."[5] These actions silenced discussion but only dampened support for reincarnation.

The Roman Catholic inquisitions between the twelfth and sixteenth centuries made more effective, zealous attempts to stamp out belief in rebirth. After thousands of fellow Christians were declared "heretics" and persecuted, the reincarnationists fled the Church and formed secret orders such as the Rosicrucians and the Freemasons.

But why was the medieval Church so antagonistic

to reincarnation? Geddes MacGregor, distinguished emeritus professor of philosophy, speculates that reincarnation probably threatened the power and authority of the Church. Because it focuses so intently on the role of the individual, he notes, reincarnation "has a special tendency to cause those who believe in it to feel able to dispense with the institutional aspects of the Christian Way."[6] In other words, if you assume responsibility for your own spiritual progress, you needn't look to another authority for guidance, absolution, and a proprietary path to salvation.

The medieval period and its enforced restrictions finally gave way to the Renaissance and an "emancipation of minds." People rediscovered Plato and Pythagoras, and popular schools of thought grew around their philosophies, including their ideas about reincarnation, which enjoyed its own rebirth of popularity.

The enlightenment of the eighteenth century brought further support of reincarnation, from such esteemed thinkers as the French philosopher Voltaire and the Swedish religious leader Swedenborg. The German Transcendentalists Kant, Hegel, Herder, Goethe, Schiller, and Richter greatly influenced the Transcendentalist movement growing in Europe and America.[7]

The American Transcendentalists of the nineteenth century, led by Emerson and Thoreau, were also influenced by Asia.[8] Eastern works such as the Bhagavad-Gita and the Upanishads, Vedas, and Puranas were translated into English, further fueling the reincarnation fires burning in America.

Henry Wadsworth Longfellow, who had an extensive library of Eastern books, wrote:

> Thus the seer,
> With vision clear,
> Sees forms appear and disappear,
> In the perpetual round of strange,
> Mysterious change
> From birth to death, from death to birth,
> From earth to heaven, from heaven to earth;
> Till glimpses more sublime,
> Of things unseen before,
> Unto his wondering eyes reveal
> The Universe, as an immeasurable wheel
> Turning forevermore
> In the rapid and rushing river of Time.[9]

Today, reincarnation is experiencing yet another surge of interest among people from a wide variety of religions and cultures, professions and economic backgrounds throughout the Western world. Why now?

Geddes MacGregor offers this answer:

We find over and over again the reincarnationist motif asserting itself just at those junctures in human history in which the institutional element in religion has become stultifying and the need for spiritualization enters. This indeed may be one of those periods in the long story of humanity.[10]

Religious experts currently attest to a growing dissatisfaction in the United States with conventional Judeo-Christian doctrines. People are searching for spiritual alternatives, and channeling is one of them.

DEEPER QUESTIONS DEMAND DEEPER ANSWERS

Many people are asking questions about life and themselves that can't be answered by the religions they currently practice. They are questions you may be asking yourself, such as "Why am I here?" or "What is my purpose in life?"

These people are turning to channels to help them find the answers. And you can too.

Because all souls' thoughts and actions are recorded in the Akashic Records at the superconscious level of mind, and channels can read those records, they can offer each of you an otherwise unattainable view of your past, present, and future.

From this broad perspective, channels can help you identify your life purpose and show you why you chose it; in other words, how your present purpose evolved from lessons learned or not learned in the past. For example, a woman who resented her constraining life as a farm wife might choose a new life conducive to freedom and self-expression. Or a soldier who tortured and killed his enemies in one life might choose to learn compassion through a life of servitude in the next.

Because past life events help shape the conditions in your life today, but you don't remember them, channels can act as your detectives. They can trace your present attributes or afflictions to your thoughts or actions in the past. They can reveal unrecognized abilities and uncover unknown obstacles. So you can nurture your talents and overcome your fears.

For example, channel Joan Morton describes a case where a client's most recent past life depicted him as a young German soldier during World War I. Secretly opposed to fighting, he tried to desert during a battle. But he was engulfed in a wave of mustard gas and died.

On hearing this story, Morton's client began to sob. He explained that in this life he had been a soldier in the Korean War. Part of his training required that he wear a gas mask. But when he did, he freaked out and collapsed, unexplainably. The experience had haunted him ever since and, inwardly, he had thought of himself as a coward. The channel's insight into his previous life experience shed light on this confusing situation and freed him of his self-condemnation.

The past can also offer fresh insight into the dynamics of present relationships. "In their interactions, people are often living out old issues, angers, or hostilities on an unconscious level," notes Morton. Simply bringing those to the surface where they can be understood and dealt with can help people tremendously. If that is not enough, channels often recommend specific actions, such as seeking a certain social environment, learning a new skill, or obtaining traditional psychological or family counseling.

Channels can peer into the future, too, and help you take advantage of potential circumstances. By considering probabilities based on your present and past decisions, channels can predict new career or life opportunities for you. When forecasting the future, channels consider how your new decisions fit into—and enhance—the whole picture of you. For example, they can show you how an individual change, such as a career move, reflects a bigger change in your value system. Or how such a move might provide new lesson material to further your progress along your particular life path.

Channels can help people clarify life issues that confuse them and deepen their self-understanding, and they can also provide historical facts, make detailed medical prescriptions, give scientific explanations of physical and other processes, locate lost objects or persons, predict future events, and identify business opportunities.

In the next two chapters, you will learn about some specific ways in which channeling has benefited two different people. You will see a business executive consider career alternatives for himself and marketing strategies for his company. And you will set out with a musician to solve a very earthly crime—only to discover the heretofore concealed door to her spiritual path.

4. The Case of the Misguided Career

Man can learn nothing unless he proceeds from the known to the unknown.

CLAUDE BERNARD

"There's only so much effort I have to exert in my life and I don't feel like wasting it on dead ends," says Tyler Stack, a chief financial officer at a high-technology firm. "If a channel can tell me which of my goals has the greatest probability for success, I feel more productive in that pursuit."

A conservative middle-aged executive, Stack has been seeking spiritual guidance in personal and business matters for a little over a year now. Before that, he says, "I never even knew what a channel did. In fact, I viewed the whole subject as rather sinister."

Until two years ago when, at a friend's encouragement, Stack visited a spiritual counselor for the first time. "I went on a lark," he recalls, "but I had hit rock bottom, so no risk appeared unreasonable at that point in my life."

For years, Stack had reveled in the heady environment of high-technology. Steadily and successfully he had climbed the corporate ladder, progressing from middle management in a large corporation to the top ranks of a fledgling computer company.

He had enjoyed the climb and the accompanying rewards of cash and status. His start-up was riding the crest of the computer wave and it promised to catapult his career—and his bank account—to new heights.

But, suddenly, the wave crashed. Along with dozens of other computer start-ups, his company went under. And so did he.

"I had never experienced a professional failure before," recalls Stack painfully. "And, worse, I felt personally responsible for all the employees we had let down."

Stack's self-confidence was shaken and his livelihood threatened. So when another company dangled an executive position before him, he hastily jumped at the opportunity. But he jumped into a nightmare.

In personality and professional style, Stack and his authoritative new boss clashed. A brief battle ensued but after six months, Stack was back on the streets, unemployed. "I was depressed and trying to scramble," he says. But this time, he didn't jump again. He opted instead for a vacation, so he could do some soul searching before he made his next move.

When he returned, Stack hesitantly agreed to seek intuitive counsel. He certainly needed help to guide him during this transition period, so he figured "Why not?" On recommendations from a trusted friend, he visited light-trance channel Joan Morton.

"She read the personal and career circumstances of

my past perfectly," says Stack. "And her predictions, many of which I could not accept at the time, have since come true." The results of that reading and consequent ones have turned Stack into a strong supporter of the sixth sense.

Here are some excerpts from Morton's first reading for Stack, followed by his reactions:

JOAN MORTON: You are closing the door on your past and preparing for a new start within the same field. I place you in finance and computers. You do best when working in an autonomous way, running your own show. But as a result of having your cage rattled, there is an issue of security bothering you. You're a little afraid now, so secretly you feel you need structure to protect you. Consequently, you may be tempted to go back to a company with lots of structure and a secure base.

But you have to let go of structures that are inhibiting. You need to take charge of your reality and trust the spark of the divine within you. Allow yourself to take risks and to be open. You will become more self-directed and more motivated.

You should work for a corporation only if you can command a "long leash"—so you can maintain a great deal of autonomy without having anyone tell you to do this, do that.

TYLER STACK: Morton's reading suddenly pulled my thoughts and confusion together and put them in perspective. I realized then that I didn't need to work for a big company, a move that I was strongly considering for the reasons she stated. I had been gravitating back to the womb where someone could take care of me.

The reading reinforced the little voice within me that was telling me not to make that move, but to look for the "right" job instead. One week after the reading, I found that job. A medium-sized corporation offered me a position where I could really be my own man—within a strongly financed company that was full of opportunity.

It was a terrific choice. And I didn't realize at the time how much of my own boss I would be. The position has placed me at the top ranks of the totem pole where I now work side-by-side with the president.

JOAN MORTON: I see you staying within the same career context, but shifting your way of dealing with people, so your interactions will be on a more meaningful level.

I sense an energy pattern where you are opening up on an emotional level. You've been open for a long time on an intellectual level, but this new pattern is heart energy. You're well-grounded, practical, with a good business head and solid management experience. But now you will be willing to allow the receptive, intuitive side of yourself to manifest.

For many years, you have felt like an imposter—putting one face on the surface and hiding your real face. You let the world see one side of you but not the other.

But now you'll allow yourself to accept your sensitive side, your feminine or "yin" self. Each of us has to accept the other part of ourselves. There's a sense of you finally coming together. And giving yourself permission to be true to who you really are. When you do that, you'll be able to express yourself in a more loving manner.

As you allow your feelings and integrity to manifest, you'll find your employees' response will be one of trust and security. They'll have more faith in what you have to offer. They'll feel more nurtured by you.

TYLER STACK: A plaque on my wall quotes Nathaniel Hawthorne from *The Scarlet Letter:* "No man, for any considerable period, can wear one face to himself and another to the multitude, without finally getting bewildered as to which may be the true."

During most of my career, I was not allowed to express my feelings. I worked in hard-driving and emotionless corporate environments, where sentimental displays were frowned upon. So I presented a different face professionally. Only some people knew the real me, the warm person behind that face. But when my start-up crumbled, I became openly emotional. It was OK to show feelings then because it went with the turf.

Now I realize that managers get much further with their employees if they're compassionate. I've learned how to integrate my professional and emotional sides better.

Oh, sometimes I still get irritated, because being considerate takes time. I may have to take a more circuitous route to solving a problem. And I'd rather bulldoze my way straight to the answer. But I like the results better in the long run. I'm happier, and my employees are much more responsive.

People who have known me for a long time say I'm entirely different now—I'm much more emotional and empathetic.

Like many people, Stack initially sought intuitive counsel to help him through a tumultuous time of transition and introspection. And it did. In the years that followed, he has reaped the rewards of the insight he gained back then. With ambition and motivation for natural energy, Stack is traveling full steam ahead on his new career track.

He continues to seek intuitive counsel periodically. But now he has broadened his areas of inquiry. "Two years ago," says Stack, "I was skeptical about intuitive counseling and limited it to my personal concerns. But now that I'm more comfortable with the process, I seek directional advice for my business too—like economic conditions and marketing strategies for new products. I use it mostly to confirm what my own gut is telling me we should do."

Here are some excerpts from more recent career and business-related readings:

JOAN MORTON: There are some choices here that you will have to look at in terms of your career. There is a change ahead of you with options. You can stay in your present job and wear two hats, or you can choose one of those jobs and wear more than two hats. I know you wield a good deal of power now, but I feel an increase. You have a lot of responsibility but not as much power as you might need.

I feel something with even more autonomy—a shift that will mean a lateral move and a step up. There's no gap in between; you won't be jobless.

TYLER STACK: At the time, I was holding two jobs, or in Joan's words, wearing two hats. I was chief financial officer and also acting general manager. I was offered my choice of which position I wanted. I chose the general manager job because it offered me a better career path to the top. Although it held no pay increase, it meant a promotion of position and responsibility.

Now as general manager I am responsible for sales and profits, managing people, planning products. Although as chief financial officer I had a lot of authority, this job gives me more "real" power—organizational-chart power. Essentially, I'm running the business.

JOAN MORTON: Your company is having a bit of a rough time now. It feels unstable but not failing. "Teetering" is the word I get. As I talk in metaphors, you need to convert them to your financial semantics. The company seems to be doing all right for now, but it needs some fresh blood and fresh ideas. I see the company becoming more stable—increasingly so under your stewardship.

TYLER STACK: At that time, my company was indeed "teetering." Sales were down the last quarter but the balance sheet looked good—as long as that last quarter didn't repeat itself. Morton talked about new blood, and the company had just hired a new president. Under the old president, the company hadn't developed any new products. When its old products hit the end of their sales cycle, there was only one new product to pick up the slack. So we got caught in a rut.

JOAN MORTON: Your company's new product is "adaptable" and "compatible" with more than one computer system. It's good quality and will make

inroads. You need to market it to people who talk
with other people who have different computers.
They'll be in a position to say, "Have you tried
this? It's compatible with this or that system."

I feel that it would be more successfully mar-
keted by word of mouth than a media blitz, so you
may not want to put all your money in advertising.
Word of mouth, people telling people, is what will
sell it. And the product will do well and make a lot
of money.

TYLER STACK: The product is compatible with computer systems of any kind: IBM, DEC, and others.
And we are now successfully marketing the product by "word of mouth." Instead of sinking money
into advertising, we're promoting the product
through PR (public relations) efforts. Specifically
we're using testimonials in our articles, quoting
what individuals say about the product. That marketing strategy is working very well.

Stack says intuitive counseling is only beginning to
be used and accepted in the business community. And
even when it is, people do not openly discuss it. "First
of all," says Stack, "it's not the kind of thing that comes
up easily in a conversation. To tell someone you're
going to a channel is almost out in the realm of something else. Most people couldn't come to grips with
that."

Unfortunately, many businesspeople still put channels in that broad category of palm readers and fortune tellers, he says. But that may change. "It's comparable to how chiropractors have elevated themselves to a level of professionalism, whereas twenty years ago they were one step above quacks."

And many people view such counsel as "private," he notes. "People don't object to talking about their religion or their political beliefs, but most people don't want to share their 'private' life. And channeling falls somewhere in that spectrum."

But he still recommends intuitive counseling to his close friends and colleagues, although he does admit to "backing" into such conversations in a way that he can back out real quick if they're shocked. "I bring the subject up," he laughs. "If the person runs with it, I know they're up to speed. Then I proceed to the next level and we share our experiences with channeling."

5. The Case of the Missing Violin

Such as the meeting soul may pierce,
In notes with many a winding bout
Of linked sweetness long drawn out.
Untwisting all the chains that tie
The hidden soul of harmony.

JOHN MILTON

Delia Moravia wept quietly, mourning the loss of her precious violin. In her mind, the elderly musician pictured the instrument's smooth flowing curves and heard its pure, soulful sound. Her heart ached as though a close friend had suddenly disappeared. Indeed, one had. This violin had been her constant companion for twenty years of grueling morning rehearsals and joyous evening performances in the symphony—until it was stolen from the locked trunk of her car while she enjoyed a carefree dinner with a friend.

That the violin would fall victim to thievery was not surprising. The 240-year-old instrument was handcrafted in Cremona, Italy, the town famous for creating unique instruments such as the Stradivarius. Over the twenty years Moravia had owned the rare violin, its monetary value had increased dramatically. And since the number of string players exceeded the number of good instruments, the violin's marketability had increased as well.

Appreciating its commercial value, Moravia had always insured the violin. But since she'd retired, she kept the violin in her home most of the time, which was equipped with a burglar alarm. So she had dropped the coverage to 50 percent.

Following the violin's theft, Moravia tried every traditional route to uncovering clues about the stolen instrument. She worked closely with the insurance company's detective. And she personally hired a private eye to conduct a separate investigation at the same time. Both investigators turned up not one clue regarding the theft or the instrument's whereabouts.

In the meantime, the shock of such a personal loss took a strenuous toll on the elderly musician. "It was very difficult to deal with the police and all those phone calls from the newspapers and radio stations," she recalls wearily. "I was constantly running back and forth between the police station and the insurance company."

Moravia was also terribly frustrated by the insurance company's casual attitude and lack of compassion. "They didn't care one hoot about getting my instrument back," she says angrily. "They were happy to pay out thousands of dollars instead."

After several stressful weeks, her already precarious health took a turn for the worse. "My interior gave me some severe warnings that enough was enough," says Moravia. "So I stopped everything." Although she insisted she didn't want the money—she wanted her violin—the insurance company sent her a settlement check anyway. The conditions stated that if she ever found the violin herself, she must return the money.

During this tumultuous time, Moravia wondered if a psychic might be able to see through the cloud of mystery surrounding the theft of her violin. A local doctor suggested she call the Center for Applied Intuition in San Francisco. Although she had never before sought psychic counsel, she was willing to try anything that might shed some light on this perplexing event.

CAI director William Kautz consequently selected deep-trance channel Jon Fox, who channels the entity Hilarion, for Moravia's reading. And he conducted the inquiry for her.

The reading unraveled like an Agatha Christie mystery, with unforeseen events taking place at every turn in the seemingly simple whodunit.

And while Fox's reading uncovered details regarding the valuable violin's theft, it did not supply the expected solution to the crime. Rather, it surprisingly explained why a solution was exactly what Moravia might *not* want to discover. Instead of trying to find the culprits and retrieve the stolen violin, the reading advised, Moravia might focus on the event's overall significance and its impact on her life.

The reading forced Moravia to look at this event—

and herself—from a broader, more spiritual perspective. It discussed specific life lessons connected with the violin. And it described how this distressful event could be transformed into a benevolent opportunity for her—to pass on a musical legacy and to grow in greater self-understanding.

Here are some excerpts from Kautz's inquiry of deep-trance channel Jon Fox, with a concluding commentary by Moravia:

JON FOX/HILARION: Greetings. This is that energy or vibration or being you call Hilarion. Before you proceed with questions on this matter of importance, it would be beneficial to visualize a clear, protective bubble of light around you, Bill, and Jon at this moment. And since you have spoken with her, Bill, please imagine that you see Delia Moravia here as well. So the three of you share this bubble of light. As you imagine it, the bubble becomes a dense compaction of potent and powerful energy. That energy will assist the specificity of this reading and help clarify the directions of Delia's life.

Now, let us begin with the questions.

WILLIAM KAUTZ: Thank you, Hilarion. We ask your cooperation to help Delia locate and retrieve a valuable violin that has been lost or stolen from her. This violin is not only expensive, but is a special possession for her. It is approximately 240 years old. Here is our principal question: "Where is this violin now and how might she retrieve it?"

JON FOX/HILARION: To ask a question from such limited perspective would force us to deny the answer. The difficulty here is that others are involved in this work, although they are not consciously known to Delia. They, too, are important here. Therefore, this is a difficult matter. It is a simple matter to speak of the violin's location, but if you retrieved it certain other people would be harmed in the process.

However, if you are presented with the full picture surrounding this theft, you might make a more intelligent and loving decision as to which course of action to pursue. That decision could then be made out of a willingness to help yourself and others involved with this lesson.

WILLIAM KAUTZ: Then let us start with the broader question of why this event has occurred in Delia's life at this particular time. What is its significance?

JON FOX/HILARION: This event took place because this legacy, this instrument that had absorbed her vibrations—and not just those of a musical nature, but of her understanding from inside of the great works of music, the virtuosity in life or perhaps we could call it the "song of the universe"—needed to be passed on in Delia's lifetime so others could benefit.

Several opportunities had attempted to present themselves in Delia's life before the theft of the violin. In certain cases these were subtle efforts of other beings to help her own guides; in other cases, they involved more direct contact with the public. Circumstances could have taken a different course had Delia consciously recognized the way music deeply affects her soul, had she brought her awareness into the world and shared it. For example, she might have given or sold the violin to someone who could benefit by its vibrations.

Or she might have shared her awareness through teaching. Within certain individuals there is the capacity to teach music and to share the inner experience of this resonance. They have the opportunity to share something very beautiful, very powerful, in the world. However, these things also are not easily explained. Just what is transmitted when the arms and the hands move in such a way, and when the ear listens in such a way? It is not merely the mechanics, as you know.

Teaching is an easy way to look at this issue, because in order to teach something to someone else one must fully recognize his own inner knowledge.

But these opportunities did not reach fruition for many reasons. One of these was the unwillingness of Delia to honor all this.

You see, it is as if Delia recognizes the beauty and the power with which she wields and works with music. But she has been unwilling to recognize all that she contributes to music and allow that to be shared with others.

Old patterns—as they are set in stone—can sometimes be very difficult to break. So they must be broken in some way; at least, this is the attitude many individual souls will choose in their life. Therefore, there is a certain advantage to starting afresh, so that the old patterns are broken in some way. And the person then—in this case, Delia—is allowed to see things anew.

Sometimes a person must move to a new location to appreciate home or him- or herself. He travels around the world simply to discover that all was best in his own backyard. This was one of the direct purposes for taking Delia's instrument away from her. There were many other things, of course, in the way of balancing past-life karma, where Delia, in a much darker and more difficult incarnation, struggled with theft for herself. Yet, as she has largely conquered those difficulties, they are being returned to her only in ways that can benefit many at once.

So it was necessary for this violin to be passed

on for others to receive her vibrations, just as Delia had received those musicians' vibrations who possessed the instrument before her. Should she have died and then this instrument been passed on, there would be far less likelihood that those who would best receive it would do so in the proper time.

Now this is an interesting point of view, because it is *not* saying that Delia has done anything wrong. There is no blame. But by putting attention on the new music, on all levels by which music is brought through, Delia can comprehend the soul-to-God connection by which this beautiful set of sound sequences comes through an individual.

You see, when a musician *becomes* the music, a certain immediacy and involvement occurs that is very much like channeling. This is easily measured in what you might call a theta brain wave state, or some matching of vibration and resonance with the various musical patterns. It is a connection to a cosmic source. As that source of energy, as that vibration moves through an individual, it is in some way transformed by the individual. So he or she may say egotistically, "I have added to the music. I have created something with it. There is something in me that has made this music special." This is a natural thing for musicians to say, since the music has come from their hands or mouth. And since people praising their work declare them to be great musicians, this is an easy trap to fall into.

But in a spiritual understanding, in an awareness of God, one recognizes that these sources are universal, regardless of what one critic might say, or a person might say, in praise of a musician's work.

But anything that blocks such a connection between an individual and God, especially toward the latter years, may be detrimental to self-understanding and carry over to the next life.

And after all, a physical instrument, the violin itself or anything of the physical world, is not terribly important in the overall scheme of things. It is what you learn of it, where you understand the deep connection with God.

So Delia can still play her music. She can still grow and understand and work with music. But she is being told at this time to do that with a new violin—so she will then recognize her vibrations as she puts them into it. If she becomes more aware of them, she will have something to pass on more consciously to others, or perhaps to write or speak about.

You see, it is important that her understanding be shared somehow, someway. Even if she simply looks at the issue more deeply, she will attain the penetrating ability to see the essence of things, the spark by which music is created—creativity itself. This is what is to be learned here.

WILLIAM KAUTZ: Let me check my concept of what seems to be the main point: Delia is at the time of her life when she needs to acknowledge and appreciate that she was working with higher sources in producing this music and not merely doing it herself. Is that a fair and accurate statement?

JON FOX/HILARION: It is, and an interesting summary. In this recognition, other doors open and she can begin her journey. Therefore, it is possible for Delia to let things be, to let this musical instrument fall into the hands of those to whom it is directed. To this end, certain specifics can be given.

The violin has been in Cincinnati and Delaware, and has made its way into the New York area. There it has found its way into the arms of a rather young child. If one wished to search and dig it out, then there would be very interesting karmic response. Delia would have to make some interesting choices here. She would have to make a clear and powerful decision to retrieve that violin—and thus prevent this young girl from learning and gaining from the vibrations that Delia has put into it.

If, however, Delia chooses to find the violin later, after it has been used welcomingly, lovingly, by another, she will assist rather than hinder the process at hand by taking away the instrument. If this child is to grow and learn from this experience, it is not necessary for Delia to be in contact with her at all. The girl will discover the violin's vibrations herself. Perhaps Delia could send a few notes about the violin, musical interpretations, or some expressions of her affinity and love of the great musicians of the past. She could even say a prayer or two for the child's continued success.

Anything along such a line would be a great help here. It would assist Delia in her own self-development as well. When Delia finally gives up the violin as lost, there will be a "letting go." This journey that we have spoken of will then be more easily begun.

WILLIAM KAUTZ: But does Delia have a responsibility first to set past things right by identifying and prosecuting people or perhaps collecting on insurance?

JON FOX/HILARION: There will certainly be no difficulty about collecting on insurance. However, in terms of prosecuting those at fault here, we see very little to be gained by Delia's involvement with the law. It is likely that the persons responsible for the theft will suffer many interesting and difficult circumstances anyway. Several of them have already fallen into difficult times—jail and the like. So prosecution would seem unnecessary.

It would also reduce Delia's ability to forgive. This forgiveness is a magnetic light that will quickly and powerfully draw this new journey—this new appreciation, this process of musical enrapturement—to her. So forgiveness is very important to her lesson here.

The karmic ongoing problem requires that at some point a sign or signal be given to the one who has "gotten the ball rolling" or sent the karma on up the chain. Therefore, Delia herself must, by the simple rule of things, eventually be given some hard evidence that this violin is being used well or that there is someone who is gaining by it. So she will know this entire journey has truly benefited another human being.

This will be the fruit that is borne of this inquiry. To know that this knowledge is ahead, and to be able to recognize it when it is there, is important. It is not necessary to look for it, but simply hearing our words may be sufficient to alert her to this possibility. But for now, she needs only to let go, look more deeply into this incident, and use it as a springboard into her new journey.

WILLIAM KAUTZ: What specific steps would help her get off to good start on this matter of letting go?

JON FOX/HILARION: The first would be in using her playing as meditation in a more directed and specific manner. She can choose a favorite piece to listen to or, preferably, play. In the middle of the piece, as the mind disassociates itself from earthly events, and the music is allowed to come through as clearly and beautifully as possible, it is time for a seed thought to be planted. This is an interesting technique and should be done gently. To make the meditation work best, the seed thought should be a singular thing—for instance, the singular idea of welcoming consciously all new ideas about music.

There are many important ideas to be considered and meditated on, but Delia has her own mind and must be free to choose them herself.

DELIA MORAVIA'S COMMENTARY

DELIA MORAVIA: When I first heard the reading, I had no trouble accepting the circumstances it described. It sounded crazy enough to be possible. That the violin had traveled through a couple of cities across the country before landing in New York made sense. When people have a hot instrument, they keep it underground and pass it around.

But when Hilarion explained how the girl needed the violin and suggested I forgive and forget—that was hard to accept. I thought, "Heck, I need it too." At first I still wanted to know its whereabouts. I thought maybe I'd ask Mr. Fox to see if that person really liked it after a few months, but I didn't. I gave up on it.

Now I realize it was a very good thing that the violin was stolen from me. And I really do believe someone has the violin who appreciates what a gem it is. It's important to me that she knows how to treat it and take care of it.

But the most important result of the violin's theft is the impact it has had on my life. It has turned me around completely, back to front, and that's good. Nothing else could have forced me to change my old patterns. For years, I worked compulsively and continually blamed myself for not being good enough. I pushed myself awfully hard—physically, because the violin is such a hard instrument to play, and mentally, because of all the stress involved.

My health had gone down steadily from too much pressure. My stomach had been miserable for years. I'd gotten down to 94 pounds and felt tired all the time. I'd seen doctor after doctor who couldn't tell me what was wrong. They'd just give me tests and X-rays on this end and that end, and say, "No, nothing wrong." Then they'd prescribe medicine for my stomach.

Now I play what I call my "picnic fiddle." And I've stopped criticizing myself. The disappointment about the theft has disappeared and I'm learning to forgive. I have a good psychotherapist who has listened to the reading and helps me work on the key issues described. And Dr. Kautz suggested that I might want to get an additional reading from channel Mary Reins, who specializes in health problems. She was extremely helpful and recommended specific diet changes.

Incidently, I have a doctor friend who diagnoses hard cases for other physicians across the country. I solicited advice from him and his diagnosis and recommendations coincided perfectly with Reins's.

So I've changed my diet and thrown away all the medicines. I'm full of pep now, and I feel great. I'm trying to meditate, although I'm not too good at it yet. But I'll keep practicing.

I feel happier, and I think that will increase. And, most importantly, I understand myself better. I'm so glad I've gotten rid of the old junk so many of us carry around. I feel relieved. And lighter in spirit somehow.

6. Expert Intuitives: A New Breed of Psychic Professionals

When other kids were putting together model airplanes, I was studying ESP.

KEVIN RYERSON

Joan Morton steered Tyler Stack's career in a more rewarding direction. And Jon Fox revealed an intricate and promising spiritual path for Delia Moravia.

In these true stories, highly skilled channels expertly penetrated their clients' problems and proffered astute new dimensions of insight and understanding. But such profound and positive rewards are not always reaped from channeling, because not all channels are so highly skilled.

In the United States alone, practitioners of the intuitive arts offering their services these days number in the thousands. Their business cards bear a multitude of titles: psychic advisor, clairvoyant, intuitive consultant, spiritual counselor, channel, metaphysician, astrologer, numerologist, trance medium, mystic, psychic healer, and more. Fees for their spiritual services run the gamut, ranging from about $20 to $500 per hour.

To date, because society and science have been reluctant to recognize intuition as a valid field of study, no criteria have been established for psychic practitioners, in contrast to the very specific requirements established for professionals in fields such as medicine and psychology. Consequently, there are no minimum qualifications for channels. And their levels of expertise vary as widely as their titles, services, and fees.

So how do you know where to turn if you wish to seek *competent* spiritual counsel? How can you ensure your experience with a channel will be a rewarding one?

You can begin by considering the advice offered in this book. The staff at the Center for Applied Intuition has been studying the phenomena of intuitively derived information for more than fifteen years, using teams of channels for scientific research, as well as individual channels for personal counseling. During that time, they have screened dozens of talented channels for accuracy and integrity. And they have established a set of criteria to distinguish "expert intuitives" from channels less skilled.

In this chapter, as well as the next, we want to share their insights about what intuitive skills and personal traits characterize expert intuitives. We will recommend several highly skilled channels and provide advice on how to find others.

SEARCH FOR AN EXPERT

Seeking intuitive counsel is only one of many paths you may choose to travel along your spiritual journey. But with an expert intuitive at your side, it may prove to be a valuable shortcut to your ultimate destination of self-understanding. To choose the best channel for your guide, you need to exercise the same care that you would in selecting any kind of self-help counseling or professional service.

For example, how do you pick your doctor, psychologist, tax consultant, or car mechanic? Most likely, you take into account personal recommendations or referrals; your understanding of their profession and their position within it; what you know about their background and personality; and, last but not least, what your intuition tells you—how your gut reacts to meeting them. You can apply the same considerations to choosing a channel.

But before you can cast your final vote, you need a potential candidate or two. So, to begin with, how do you find an expert intuitive?

Responding to advertisements might be one way. But relying on them for your only source of referral can be confusing and potentially dangerous. At best, advertisements are informative introductions. At worst, they are misleading assemblies of hyperbole, with no clear indication of what lies behind them. For example, look at the following two advertisements and where they might lead you. First, an advertisement in a metaphysical directory states subtly, "Life path counseling and intuition training from a gifted, spiritual clairvoyant."Second, in a local newspaper, another advertisement boasts blatantly, "Psychic will solve all love, marriage, business problems." And for extra enticement: "Readings half-price this week."

Answering the first advertisement might carry you to a contemporary office or home where a channel would skillfully provide the type of spiritual counsel described in this book. But answering the second could draw you to a dark room with beaded drapes, where Madame Zola would dramatically cast your fortune while gazing over a crystal ball.

So you can see that all psychic practitioners who promote themselves are not necessarily expert intuitives. In fact, most of the best channels advertise very little or not at all. Instead, they rely on their reputation to promote themselves.

You stand a better chance of finding competent channels through referrals—from a trusted friend or an experienced organization like the Center for Applied Intuition.

Once you've found some candidates, try them out. Compare their personal traits and experience to the description of expert intuitives given here.

Competent channels come from every walk of life, representing the whole spectrum of human interests from the humblest to the most urbane. They are construction workers, aerospace engineers, housewives, psychologists, roofers, electronics engineers, writers, hypnotherapists, artists, and corporate executives. Sprinkled across the country, with a heavy concentration on the West Coast, they range in age from twenty to over sixty. They are simple and sophisticated, uneducated and intellectual, fat and thin, quiet and vivacious.

When they first discovered their channeling ability and how long they worked at its development varies greatly, even among the best channels. For example, when he was seven years old Edgar Cayce saw and talked with "visions." By age twenty-one, with only a eighth-grade education behind him, this deeply religious mystic began his astounding forty-year channeling career.[1]

And here are some more contemporary examples: After studying metaphysics for several years, twenty-two-year-old Kevin Ryerson first channeled John and Tom McPherson during a meditation. During the decade and a half since then, he has devoted himself to sharing spiritual messages from higher planes with people here on earth.

While practicing self-hypnosis at age thirty, Jon Fox, an electrical engineer with no previous psychic inclination, first channeled Hilarion. With little further training, he began deep-trance channeling for individuals and groups.

After almost seven years of attending trance classes, twenty-eight-year-old Lin David Martin began to experience the light-trance process, or as he calls it, "clairvoyant channeling." In two more years, he experienced the deep-trance process as well. Now teachers from another level of consciousness impart spiritual information via Martin to individuals and groups throughout the United States and Europe.

Some channels were aware of their psychic powers in childhood but didn't find it "acceptable" to acknowledge and practice them until adulthood. Or they didn't discover their intuitive aptitude until later in life, during a time of spiritual growth or even personal need.

Joan Morton, for instance, first experienced her psychic powers at thirty, while praying in a convent following the death of her fiancé. And Charles Nunn, a successful businessman, didn't acknowledge his spiritual calling until serious illnesses presented him with five near-death experiences. Then he began channeling and "got so healthy he forgot to die." Today he enjoys excellent health and practices intuitive consulting all over the world.

On the surface, the collective profiles of these expert intuitives form a "crazy quilt"—a patchwork of personalities, ages, and appearances. However, several common inner threads run throughout their lives. Highly skilled channels are all devoted individuals who have deliberately refined their intuitive skills to a high level of expertise. Motivated to help humanity, they practice their intuitive profession with integrity and a genuine concern for their clients' spiritual growth.

COMMON EXPERIENCE: INTENSE INNER EVOLVEMENT

Expert intuitives have all undergone some form of experiential or instructional training. As a first step, each decided, consciously or subconsciously, to discover more about his or her life purpose and how best to fulfill it. During the ensuing period of self-development, these spiritual students learned to tap the vast source of inner knowing available to everyone who pursues it with enough dedication.

Some began channeling before any instructional programs were available, as they are today. They taught themselves to channel primarily through books and extensive intuitive practice. Others trained with individual teachers who informally acted as their guides or support persons. Others attended privately organized daily or weekly classes on developing intuition—the type of workshops that are becoming more common today.

And some channels even completed structured instructional programs in such areas as parapsychology, spiritual development, and transpersonal counseling.

Mary Reins, for example, participated in a two-year experiential program at the Kansas City School of Metaphysics. Ryerson attended a two-year course of studies at the University of Life institution in Phoenix, Arizona, where he received accreditation and a teaching credential. He also later attained accreditation and theological credentials from the Universal Life Alliance in Tempe, Arizona. Martin completed the same intensive curriculum at the University of Life as Ryerson, and continued to teach at that institution for several years. And Nunn received a bachelor's degree in humanistic parapsychology from the Arthur Ford International Academy of Mediumship in North Carolina.

Whatever their amount or type of training, these expert intuitives learned to skillfully set aside subconscious blocks and fears in order to open the kind of clear intuitive channel to the superconscious described in an earlier chapter. (Chapter 9 delves into the process of developing intuition in greater depth.)

But even after training, most of these channels did not immediately convey scientific, business, or other objective information. First, they found themselves channeling information for their family and friends. In relaying that information and soliciting feedback, they gradually gained valuable experience, which led into a formal practice of intuitive counseling.

Such a period of internship is important for channels because practice improves their confidence and refines their skills. It also teaches them how to adeptly handle the numerous challenges clients may present during readings. For example, some clients can be very skeptical, even hostile. They may try to test the channel. Others, while ambiguous about what they really want to know, have firm expectations about what they want to hear. They may strongly contest or reject what the channel tells them. And still others may try to unload emotional problems on their channel.

Consequently, in the face of such challenges, channels need to maintain personal objectivity and stay "grounded" in order to provide intuitive guidance that is sound, accurate, and relevant. Such a complex task requires an astute combination of abilities strengthened by experience.

EXPERTISE ENHANCES COMMUNICATION

Most skilled channels are capable of addressing any area of inquiry. But some channels, like doctors or lawyers, have found they are more interested in one aspect of intuitive counseling than in others. Some specialize in spiritual matters; others opt for career guidance, health consultation, or past-life recall. And some like to work with all aspects.

The entities that come through deep-trance channels often pick their own pet topics for concentration or emphasis—perhaps personal responsibility or a special avenue of spiritual growth. And an entity's interest can vary, even be diametrically opposed, to his or her channel's. The entity Martenard, who communicates through Richard Wolinsky, once caused the channel considerable chagrin by expounding political opinions completely contrary to Wolinsky's.

Sometimes channels' preferences reflect their background and experience prior to channeling when they practiced different careers. This *does not* mean, however, that channels are incapable of channeling information outside their areas of specialty. Quite the contrary: expert intuitives can respond adequately to critical questions about virtually any subject. As a basic source of information and wisdom, they are not limited by their personal interests, education, or previous careers.

However, a particular expertise may enable a channel to communicate more clearly about a given subject. If a channel and his or her client "speak the same language," whether it's the vernacular or a professional jargon, the client may interpret and understand the reading more easily. Like often attracts like.

In accord with his technical background, Fox frequently channels Hilarion's insights into scientific or medical situations. And because he managed a manufacturing business for several years, Nunn often counsels corporate clients about business prospects and human resource issues. Of course, a match of interests or experience is not necessarily a guarantee of intuitive expertise in that area. Some skilled channels with technical backgrounds have trouble providing information straight from a higher source—without being influenced by their personal memories of their previous education or experience.

The "like-attracts-like" principle also holds true for personalities. If a client finds a channel's personality irritating or offensive—for whatever reason—those emotions could distort the client's receptivity to a reading. For instance, one conservative married man was so disturbed by his channel's obvious homosexuality that he nearly walked out in the middle of a very good reading.

There are always certain people, in any aspect of your life, with whom you communicate best. Three different channels could deliver the same information in three different ways. But you might "hear" only one of them. So although backgrounds and personalities do not affect channels' abilities to elicit intuitive information, they can pave a smoother road for interpersonal communication. And after all, intuitive counseling is a two-way street. As you conduct your search for a channel, you will find yourself on that street, pondering different channels' reputations and personalities.

To start your search, an extensive list of channels is included in the Appendix at the back of this book. However, this list is not all-inclusive. There are many other competent channels practicing their intuitive skills across the United States and throughout the world. You can find information about them in metaphysical directories or announcements in public libraries, health food stores, and specialty bookstores.

It may take more than one reading from the same channel to judge whether that man or woman has the personal traits and intuitive expertise to give you expert spiritual counsel, and to determine if the chemistry between you and the channel will enhance or hinder your relationship.

Eventually, as you learn to trust and use your own intuition, you will be able to make quicker decisions. But until then, use the information from this chapter and the criteria in the next to help you select candidates.

7. Your Role in Your Reading

> It takes two to speak the truth—one to speak and another to hear.
>
> HENRY DAVID THOREAU

"Please come with questions," requests a letter from Kevin Ryerson prior to a personal consultation. "The depth of Spirit response during the trance channeling will reflect the sincerity and the depth of your questions."

Although the channel acts as your connection to a higher source, the outcome of your reading does not rest entirely on his or her shoulders. You (the client) also play an important role in determining its successful or unsuccessful results. Your motivation, preparedness, and receptivity significantly affect your channel and your reading.

This chapter gives you a prechanneling checklist to help you examine your motives for seeking spiritual counsel. It tells you how to prepare for your first and subsequent consultations. And it provides a set of criteria you can use to evaluate channels and the intuitive counseling they deliver.

ASK YOURSELF "WHY?"

First, you need to do some soul searching of your own and honestly assess your motives for seeking channeled counsel. Research conducted at the Center for Applied Intuition has found that a client's sincere motivation and open receptivity encourage the channel and foster a free flow of high-quality intuitive information. But a client's undue skepticism, insincerity, or unethical intentions can inhibit the channel and affect the depth of information obtained. For example, channel Mary Reins explains,

If a client seeks a reading primarily for curiosity instead of personal growth, it is much harder to zero in on his core issues. It's as though he has erected a glass sheath around him which deflects some of my energy. I can still deliver accurate information, but it will not be as deep.

Improper motives can disturb, even block, the subtle connection that takes place between you and your channel. So before you seek intuitive counsel, examine your intentions. Ask yourself the following questions:

1. Are you a thrill-seeker looking for a new kick?
2. Are you searching for someone to make decisions for you?
3. Are you covertly trying to discredit psychic means of obtaining information?

4. Are you looking for a fortune teller? Someone who will casually cast your future and make decisions for you?

5. Are you trying to gain information that will give you power over other people? So you can advance your position at their expense?

6. Are you getting this reading to please your partner even though you're inwardly opposed to it?

7. Are you looking for a quick formula for instant wealth?

Or do the following questions describe you:

8. Are you searching for a deeper insight into the real *you?*

9. Do you want to know and understand your true purpose in this life?

10. Are you skeptical but open to the possibility that valid information can be obtained intuitively?

11. Are you seeking assistance through a period of personal transition in your career or a relationship?

12. Are you trying to rid yourself of confusing fears or inhibiting emotional blocks?

13. Are you investigating past-life events that may be influencing your present situation?

14. Are you searching for medical insight, and/or health or diet recommendations?

15. Are you committed to using the information you obtain to advance your spiritual growth?

If you answered yes to any of Questions 1 through 7, you need to step back and examine your reasons for seeking intuitive guidance. For although some of these questions might seem exaggerated or even appear amusing, they all exemplify really poor motives for channeling—which will backfire as they inhibit your reading.

However, if you answered yes to any of questions 8 through 15, you are demonstrating sincerity and honest intent—motives that will best enable your channel to facilitate the flow of intuitive information from a higher dimension to you.

DO YOUR HOMEWORK: SET PERSONAL GOALS AND PREPARE QUESTIONS

Now that you've examined your motives, the next step in your preparation is to establish your personal goals or objectives, as best you can. Decide what you desire most out of your reading. Write down those objectives and prepare a list of questions for your channel. Set some priorities, in case time prevents all of your issues from being addressed.

Most channels conduct their consultations, especially life readings, according to some established format. For instance, channels frequently start a reading by delivering a general discourse on the dynamics of

---

Different Types of Intuitive Consultation

Life Reading: A general discourse covering your overall life dynamics, including purpose, experiences, lessons, mental and spiritual patterns. (May include some discussion of past lives.)

Past Lives Reading: A reading devoted to exploring past lives, especially those that are influencing your present existence.

Special Inquiry: A reading focusing on a particular area of personal (mental, emotional, spiritual, or physical), business, or scientific inquiry.

---

your life, including your life purpose, your major life lessons, your current life phase or experience, and your mental and spiritual patterns. Then they open the reading up to your questions. You can then request more detailed information about subjects they've already covered. And you can ask questions about additional topics, exploring such diverse areas as interpersonal relationships, career directions, past lives, karmic patterns, personal expression, health, and spiritual guidance.

You may ask about any matter of concern to you. But prepare your questions carefully to reflect what you really want to know. Give only enough background to clarify your questions. Don't waste the channel's time—and yours—with lengthy narrations. Channels can directly access the details they most need. However, don't make them search for relevant information you already know.

Formulate your questions as clearly, simply, and specifically as you can. Vague questions tend to elicit vague answers. Lucid questions evoke lucid answers.

The Center for Applied Intuition has found that skilled channels answer sincere and well-posed questions with clarity and perception. Indeed, they often reach far beyond original queries and offer additional, deeper insight. Many times they even answer questions before they are asked!

In some exceptional instances, however, channels may refuse to answer certain questions. While their ultimate information source is virtually unlimited, channels themselves—and even their guides—work within some restrictions.

The discarnate entity John explains those restrictions through Kevin Ryerson: "Only God knows everything. We are limited to the framework in which we can aid or help people. We may divulge information that gives insight and fits the emotional context and need of a person at that time. But we do not have access to thoughts that need to be held private for an individual's life lessons or that may interfere with the learning process of another person."

Let's say a channel foresees that a man is about to undergo a personal crisis, like a marital separation or a car accident. The channel may withold this information because foreknowledge of it would detract from the very lessons the man needs to learn through that experience. (Although it is sometimes hard to appreciate the value of such crises as constructive life experiences, they are often necessary for inner growth.) Another channel might foresee that a woman is going to win the lottery next year but he (or she) doesn't tell her. With advance notice, the woman might stop trying to succeed and simply wait. Or she might begin living a lifestyle she can't yet afford.

As in any type of counseling or psychotherapy, a certain responsibility rests with the counselor to convey information that his or her client can work with effectively. Ethical channels only convey information that supports their clients' best interest, fosters their spiritual growth, and does not invade anyone else's privacy.

YOUR READING: EACH ONE IS UNIQUE

Different channels receive and deliver intuitive counsel in different ways. Some are strictly verbal. Others may use visual images instead of words, or a combination of both. For example, they may convey your life purpose or describe a particular issue in symbolic images or anecdotes.

Reins recalls an image she received while conducting a life reading for a Japanese woman:

The woman sat with her arms wrapped around her body and bound. Only her hands were untied. But they too were constricted—by burdens other people had been placing in them for centuries. Now that her hands were full and ready to collapse, she felt a strong sense of failure about dropping the weight she'd been told to carry. But, suddenly, she dropped everything anyway. And with her hands free, she untied her ropes.

From that moment on, Reins says, the Japanese woman understood that her life purpose was to help free other women bound in a similar way. She experienced a new perception of her own power, and her life changed its passive course.

So, don't be surprised if your channel takes you on a fascinating visual or verbal journey. But regardless of how the channel conducts your reading, relax and open yourself up for a unique experience. Allow yourself to feel and enjoy the energy that transpires between you and your channel during the reading. Channels say this energy comes through them from a higher source and is especially for you. Some claim the energy itself can have a mental and even physical healing effect.

Observe and listen, but don't try to analyze the information being delivered while the reading is in progress. Channels normally provide a cassette tape of each reading. (If they don't, bring your own recording equipment.) You'll have plenty of time later to analyze and evaluate your reading.

AFTER THE READING: TIME FOR EVALUATION

The best channels deliver highly accurate, complete, and relevant information when questions are properly motivated and posed—that is, when they arise from a sincere desire for knowledge, a commitment to act on the knowledge sought, and a positive ethic. But that refers to the *best* channels, not *all* channels. Many practicing channels make astounding pronouncements, but also make abundant mistakes. And even when they provide "accurate" information, it is often incomplete or misleading to the inquiry at hand. In fact, after screening dozens of channels, the Center for Applied Intuition has found that only a few practitioners of intuitive skills can meet its high criteria for credibility, accuracy, completeness, and relevance.

You, too, should be discriminating. After each reading, use the following criteria to evaluate your channel and the intuitive information you received.

CREDIBILITY

Did the channel reveal intimate insights about you and your past? Did you feel like he or she knew and understood you?

Frequently, channels begin a reading by telling you deeply personal information about your past that you but probably not many other people already know. Recounting "old information" may not be directly helpful but it can be an extremely useful way of establishing credibility, especially with spiritual novices. It tells the client, "Yes, we're zeroing in on you. We know what's going on and we truly have your best interests at heart." It establishes a basis of confidence with the client, from which the channel can slowly reach out into unexplored and sometimes sensitive realms of the person's past, present, and future.

ACCURACY

How accurate was the information provided in your reading? You will find that some parts of your reading can be validated by confirming facts or past events. And predictive information can be checked by waiting to see if the events do indeed occur.

However, other parts of your reading will not be verifiable according to the narrow rules of "scientific proof." There is no way, for example, to "prove" how your grandmother really felt about you when she was living, or how you feared criticism as a child. Ironically, almost all occurrences that are centrally important to human life are unrepeatable, uncontrollable, or nonphysical—and thus not subject to scientific methods of verification. In such cases, the information relayed can be verified only by your direct and inner experience—that is, if it rings true to you.

COMPLETENESS AND RELEVANCE

Was the information complete? Did the channel tell the full story? Or did the channel miss something really important, such as a key relationship you're having trouble with? Was the information relevant? Could it be practically applied to your present situation?

Along with accuracy and credibility, the issues of completeness and relevance most clearly distinguish the best intuitive practitioners from those less developed or experienced. Almost anyone with a little psychic ability can advertise himself or herself as a channel and gain a following of gullible clients who are amazed at a few insights, recounted past lives, or general advice that would be beneficial if followed. The highly skilled channel, however, sees the full picture, not just fragments of it, and focuses on those portions of the picture that the client can actually use.

GIVE YOUR READING TIME TO UNFOLD

The process of integrating and implementing the intuitive information you receive takes time. If you're like most people, you'll progress through four stages: first you'll open, then you'll experience, then you'll understand, and then you'll know.

Step 1: *Open* means "unfold, remove obstructions from." Once you drop barriers or beliefs that have limited your personal growth in the past, you will begin to blossom and unfold. Like an open flower draws bee after bee, you will automatically attract new life opportunities and experiences.

Step 2: *Experience* means "meet, undergo, feel, encounter." Out of every experience, high or low, wonderful or painful, you will reap new learning and understanding from your involved participation. (Remaining an observer is not enough.)

Step 3: *Understand* means "grasp the meaning, comprehend." You will process your experience with your thinking mind in terms of familiar concepts and words. But your new understanding may confront your old beliefs. So you'll need to test it before you can completely integrate it into your prior personality.

Step 4. *Know* means "perceive as fact or truth." As you augment your new understanding, you will no longer need to test it. You won't even need to explain it in rational terms. You will simply "know" what is true for you. And that knowledge, integrated into your life, will change you into a different and greater person.

Let this process take place slowly and gracefully, permeating your entire being. Learning to truly know yourself is a holistic experience—not an individual intellectual exercise like studying a new subject in school. Don't force it. Don't resist it. It will work naturally in accord with your inner personal development.

The insights and directions described in channeled readings unfold over time. And the information provided will take on new meaning as your self-understanding grows.

"Like parables, intuitive readings often deliver messages that carry various levels of meaning," says channel Penney Peirce. "As you repeat the same sentence at different times in life, its meaning changes depending on your level of growth and point of view."

Most channels encourage clients to take the tapes of their readings home, listen to them the next day and then again periodically over the next several months. Each time, they say, you'll gain a deeper understanding of the reading and yourself. Indeed, the best readings will continue to hold valuable guidance for years to come.

We hope your interaction with a channel will be a revealing and rewarding experience. If you follow the guidelines and use the criteria in this chapter, the chances are good that it will be. With sincere motivation, an open relationship with your channel, proper preparation, and careful evaluation, you will gain intuitive insights that will strongly enhance—and perhaps dramatically change—the way you live your life.

8. Your Life Is in *Your* Hands

The whole theory of the universe is directed unerringly to one single individual—namely to YOU.

WALT WHITMAN

With your channel, you have now journeyed beyond the limits of the logical mind into another dimension. And you have returned, bringing back a wealth of intuitive information about yourself. Over the next several months and even years, you will have time to reflect on, integrate, and implement that information.

But immediately after a reading, especially your first, you may feel a bit overwhelmed by the scope and intimacy of the insight provided. You may feel amazed, even slightly dazed, by the mystical process in which it was obtained. You may also be confused and wonder, "How much should psychic predictions influence my future decisions? And how do I integrate this intuitive information into my day-to-day living?"

You begin by keeping your head on your shoulders and remembering that you, and only you, control your destiny.

Use the criteria covered in the previous chapter to objectively evaluate the intuitive information you received. But don't forget to also listen to your own inner voice in determining what is "true" for you. And above all, *never* surrender your power to any other person—channel, entity, or spirit.

PROTECT YOUR POWER

Heed the words that higher sources have spoken through channels at the Center for Applied Intuition: "We are not final authorities," they have declared emphatically. "As guides, we show you options, so you can choose your path more wisely. We are here to help you broaden your own perceptions and come to know yourself better—by whatever means work best for you."

Channels are guides. Let them shine light on your path and reveal opportunities that await you. But don't ask them to dictate your lives. Channels are fountains of insightful information from which you may drink heartily. But don't let them be your only diet.

Follow the example of Dr. Gabriel Cousens, a holistic physician who views channeling as one of many valuable ways to obtain information. While conducting research for his book, *Spiritual Nutrition and the Rainbow Diet,* he sought intuitive guidance from Kevin Ryerson.

"John and Atun-Re (entities who communicate through Ryerson) were a wonderful source of information and a true inspiration," recalls Cousens. "And so was Kevin himself." But Cousens did not view either the entities or the channel as figures of authority from whom he should merely accept dictation. "Through our dynamic interaction, seed ideas and concepts arose," he says. "But it was my responsibility to get those seeds to grow." So Cousens combined the channeled information with scientific and clinical research—as well as his own inner experiences—to generate the material for his book.

Yet you should not follow the steps of the sensitive artist who grew so dependent on channel Charles Nunn that he couldn't make artistic or personal decisions by himself. "He called me three times a day, seven days a week," recalls Nunn. "At first I thought he needed my help to push him through a knothole. But the calls kept coming. So I refused further consultation, telling him he would never make it through life relying so fully on information from other people, no matter how psychic they were. Finally, he started listening to himself. And his painting took off in a wonderful new direction."

It is understandable how even intelligent individuals such as this artist could become overdependent on channeled information, especially when it concerns predictions. Natural human curiosity piques people's interest in the future. They want to know: Will I marry? When should I move, and where? Will this disease ever leave me? When is the great earthquake going to strike California? Unfortunately, a willingness to let others decide these matters for them can turn curiosity into an addiction. People's preoccupation with the future stems basically from insecurity. It, in turn, arises from the fear that something may be taken away from them, something they think they need for survival, nurturance, or happiness—in short, for maintaining their concept of who they are. Their human desire to know what the future holds becomes stronger than their will to be self-determining, to exercise the freedom to choose tomorrow what they may fear today. So they willingly give up their power to someone (or something) on whom they hang the cloak of authority. Then they become monopolized by another's predictions.

"Too often if you tell clients that something is going to happen," says channel Penney Peirce, "they expend an undue amount of psychic energy thinking about that prediction. They try to create it. Or they try to avoid it. At any rate, they miss opportunities coming in the present moment because they're fixed on some point in the future."

This doesn't mean that you shouldn't ask questions about the future, but you should regard the answers as guidance and potentiality rather than fact or destiny. And you need to realize that the future is not all predetermined or predictable anyway.

THE FUTURE: FORESEEABLE OR NOT?

People who ask a channel or a discarnate entity questions about the future are assuming, at least implicitly, that their future is knowable and therefore predictable. But if so, do individuals have any free choice in determining their future? And if not, why bother asking questions about the future at all?

Herein lies the age-old paradox of determinism and free will. On one side lies the argument for a source of higher intelligence that watches over you from a point of great perspective and knowledge. This wise source—God, the superconscious self, a guide, a discarnate being, or even a scientific authority—can supposedly see what you are going to choose before you choose it.

If you accept this simplified view of determinism, then you might as well stop struggling with difficult decisions and do whatever the source tells you. This approach requires quite a bit of faith, perhaps even gullibility, but carries some merit.

On the other side lies the belief that the future is completely free and undetermined. Although the future already exists—because all possible futures already exist, in some sense—you still get to choose the one you want.

This could be called the "you-create-your-own-reality" view because it sees the future as being continually created by the mental processes, individual and collective, of humankind. These mental processes include beliefs everyone has agreed on about what is real and what is not.

Indeed, evidence is clear that the human mind is a much stronger creator of its environment than has been commonly perceived in the past. Persons who have been privileged to experience altered states of consciousness testify to the transience of time and space. They have experienced the physical power of thoughts to move beyond their limits. They tell how they could peer through walls, move objects at will, merge with animals and objects, undergo extreme physical environments (such as walking on hot coals) without physical damage, and see distant localities, distant times, and inside others' minds.

If you accept this view, you assume a great deal of responsibility—apparently all, it seems—to fashion your own future. And you are forced to wonder if *anything* is fixed.

According to repeated readings by expert intuitives about the subject of the future, both of these positions carry some truth. They say that while some of your personal future is effectively predetermined, you still have tremendous free will with which you can create—and change—your reality.

CHARTING YOUR COURSE

Part of your present condition, the readings explain, results from decisions you have already made (consciously or unconsciously, individually or in collaboration with others) over the course of this and other lifetimes. For example, a man may think he has consciously chosen his present wife or career path. But that choice may have been largely governed by early, unconscious decisions buried deep in his mind—perhaps even prior to his birth. Or a woman blames an accident, illness, or personal loss on "fate" or "bad luck." Inwardly, however, she may have chosen that difficult ordeal to teach her a lesson she had been reluctant to learn from earlier, more gentle experiences.

So the part of present existence predetermined by past decisions is fairly fixed. However, higher sources say that none of these prior choices is completely irrevocable. "You have total free will," they say. "And you can change anything in your reality."

Unfortunately, many people travel through life blaming "circumstances" or other people for the difficulties of their existence. They avoid personal responsibility by projecting the sources of their problems on an apparently fixed environment or on other individuals whom they think they cannot change. But people actually have much more power to determine their destiny than most may think.

You've heard about the power of positive thinking. If you believe it is within your power to create or change a circumstance, *it is*—through your connection with the universal source. If you focus your energy and personal power on what you want or need and fully open yourself to receive it, the universe will manifest it for you.

As you grow in spiritual understanding, you will become more aware of how you are continually creating your own reality. Instead of simply fulfilling your destiny, you will start consciously changing your life for the better. "Once one realizes one has the power to create, the power to change one's own life, then one becomes a part of the universality of all that is," says the discarnate entity Mentor. "When one begins to play within the natural laws of manifestation, karmic debt is released."[1]

CHANNELS CAN HELP YOU FIND AND FOLLOW YOUR LIFE PATH

The question remains: How should you work with intuitive sources to best aid your personal progress? The answer is simple: Regard them as guides who can help clarify your life purpose and shed light on optional paths toward its fulfillment.

When expert intuitives tap into the higher realms of knowledge, they pick up the most probable future alternatives that lie ahead for each client. As explained earlier, these alternatives emerge naturally from what that person has already decided—consciously and subconsciously, individually and collectively—during this lifetime and others.

Sometimes a channel picks up only one likely alternative and states it accordingly. Other times, he or she may receive two or more. For example, one February a successful electronics engineer asked channel Lin David Martin when he would embark on a new personal relationship. Martin predicted, "In four or six months."

The following summer, while Martin was conducting meditation workshops in Denmark and Norway, the engineer was traveling through Europe. He tried phoning Martin so he could attend his June workshop. Martin recalls, "I had a strong psychic message that someone was trying to reach me at the time. But we missed connections." So the engineer didn't attend the first workshop. But a lovely Danish woman did.

The engineer traveled through England and then reached Norway—in time to attend Martin's August workshop. So did the Danish woman. They embarked on a whirlwind romance and married the following year. Perhaps if they had met in June, that sentimental segment of the engineer's European tour would have started two months sooner!

In some cases where a channel receives multiple options, he or she provides the one that is more encouraging and not already foreseen by the client.

Other times, a channel may pick up alternatives that would be frightening to his or her client—for example, an impending accident, a personal loss, or some other crisis that may be required to teach certain lessons. The channel may or may not communicate those alternatives, depending on how ready the client is to make a life choice that would obviate the crisis. Some channels help clients play a "what if" game. They answer hypothetical questions such as "What would happen if Mary went with this person or that job?" or "According to the energy moving now, would this approach be successful?".

When predicting a client's future, the channel assumes that the inquirer does not make any drastic changes in life direction before the predicted event takes place. Consider this simple example of how a new decision could change a previously predictable event. Say you see a man carrying a box across a parking lot. You can predict pretty reliably that he will continue carrying that box to the other side of the lot and put it in his car. But that isn't *totally* reliable because he might suddenly change his mind and run back in the other direction.

So it goes with many life decisions. Major changes in direction that would negate predictions are usually improbable, but they are always possible. So remember to regard future predictions simply as strong probabilities. Don't forget that there may be other alternatives and that *your destiny depends on your own decisions.*

Give it some thought before you beseech another person or entity to unveil your future. First, ask yourself why you want to know this information. This will help make you aware of the power inherent in your response and how you might use it. Second, ask yourself why you are seeking this help from another, instead of yourself. It's OK to be stuck, but if so, be sure to acknowledge that you are stuck. Third, consider how much credibility you will be attaching to whatever answer you are given. For example, how far are you willing to go along with what you are told?

Finally, ask yourself the same question you are about to pose to a channel and see what response you receive. Having passed through the first three steps, you may find the answer more readily accessible through your own intuitive resources. And you may find your mind more receptive for whatever answer comes through your channel.

Let channels and their guides show you the way up the mountain. But don't ask them to carry you there. They cannot change your life lessons, but they can help you see them more clearly and help you advance through them more quickly. Take advantage of their extended insight and expanded perspective to better understand your true self and your life purpose. Use channels as a second source of information, with your own inner voice being the final authority.

Always remember that *you* are the center of your universe, the creator of your own reality. Your greatest personal asset is your free will. If you apply your free will properly, according to Edgar Cayce readings, "you can change the circumstances, directions, and outcomes of events in your lives for the better."[2]

So, with channeled information in hand, focus your will on creating a better and more fulfilling life for yourself and your loved ones. Learn how to tune into your own inner sources of guidance. The next chapter begins to show you how.

9. Tune In to Channeling

Most people live, whether physically, intellectually, or morally, in a very restricted circle of their potential being. They make use of a very small portion of their possible consciousness, and of their soul's resources in general, much like a man who out of his whole body organism, should get into a habit of using and moving only his little finger.

WILLIAM JAMES

A four-year-old girl asks, "Mommy, how come Grandma is so sick today?" Her mother retorts impatiently, "Grandma's not sick, and stop being so silly." Later that day, the mother finds out that in fact Grandma had suffered a stroke and was rushed to the hospital.

A young man vacationing in Europe for the first time enters an old church and gasps. For some reason, he recognizes all the details of the stained glass windows and remembers the discomfort of sitting in the angular wood pews. But how could he? He's never been there before. He shakes his head and attributes the experience to "déjà vu."

A woman abruptly walks away from a conversation at a friend's party. She "feels something is wrong" and calls home. The babysitter reports that her infant is running a high fever and has just vomited.

An entrepreneurial executive follows his "gut hunch" and launches a controversial new product—

despite contrary advice from his financial analysts. The product and his company become an overnight success.

A child's insight, a woman's instinct, "déjà vu," and a gut hunch—all are familiar examples of how intuition leaks into people's lives every day.

Consider some more. Have you ever felt "butterflies" flutter around your stomach? Or had a terrific idea flash into your head? Or felt goose bumps rise up on your arm when you were being told the truth—or, worse, a lie?

More than likely, you have all experienced flashes of intuition, or "direct knowing," in one form at some time or another. Intuition has no prejudice. It does not make itself available to some people and not to others. Then why, you may ask, do some people seem to have so much more intuition that others?

Intuition manifests strongly for certain individuals because they have deliberately opened themselves up to the wonderful realm of the sixth sense—where understanding takes place without the effort of reasoning.

Unfortunately, most people don't choose to operate in an intuitive mode because they don't believe it holds any value for them. Their intuitive experiences as children had probably been devalued, suppressed, or even ridiculed. Or their "woman's intuition" had been passed off lightly. Or their "sensitivities" had been viewed as illogical or even "unmanly." After all,

Western society, with its heavy scientific bent, hasn't taught or even encouraged people to trust their inner sources of knowledge.

But, as noted in Chapter 1, many people have bucked familial and societal pressures and employed their "sixth sense" anyway. Throughout history, philosophers, inventors, writers, and artists have believed that life holds much more than meets the eye. They have nurtured and relied on their intuition to beget new concepts and foster their creativity. People from every sector of society are now starting to follow in their footsteps. From heeding hunches to developing channeling skills, they're learning to tap their intuition. You can, too.

We intend to outline a natural and gradual progression for refining your intuitive skills that can lead as far as channeling. Entire books could be, and have been, written about the many techniques for facilitating intuitive development and the issues that arise during that process.[1] However, the underlying principles are few and simple. In what follows, we will share these basics with you.

OPEN COMMUNICATIONS WITH YOUR INTUITIVE SOURCE

As our earlier examples show, intuitive knowledge often leaks through to people—perhaps not deliberately, but when the need or desire is strong enough.

More dramatically, intuition frequently leaks through at times of physical crisis or emotional upheaval, such as during a "near death" experience or visionary "visit" from a deceased friend or loved one.

Expert intuitives have learned to take deliberate control of the leak-through process so that superconscious knowledge can flow to consciousness in a graceful and communicative way.

In order for you to access your intuition more regularly and apply it successfully in your everyday life, you must open communications with your intuitive source, the superconscious mind. This task is not necessarily easy, because in order to reach your conscious mind, superconscious information must travel through the subconscious mind, a storehouse of memories and fears that can distort intuitive information before it reaches consciousness.

As you will recall from Chapter 2, this working model of the mind is divided into the three arenas: conscious, subconscious, and superconscious. The *conscious mind* is a device for reasoning and focusing attention. It represents that portion of total reality of which you are aware—largely experienced through your senses. The *subconscious mind* is a storehouse of impressions, feelings, fears, memories, and incomplete experiences. The *superconscious mind* is a universal reservoir of knowledge transcending time and space.

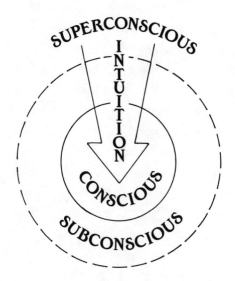

LEARNING MEANS LETTING GO

In order to be able to pull in intuitive information, you need to create a tunnel or "channel" from the superconscious mind to the conscious core. To do this, you basically need to "clean out" or "let go of" enough subconscious obstacles—such as anger, jealousy, resentment, inappropriate beliefs, negative attitudes, and other aspects of fear—to allow information to flow from the superconscious to consciousness more clearly and without distortion. Your conscious mind will then grow larger as your awareness expands.

Thus, you can see that learning to use your intuition is much different from the type of learning you're probably accustomed to. It is not a matter of acquiring new facts or learning skills that you didn't already have—as you do when you learn to speak French or play baseball. Developing intuition depends less on adding new material to your mind than on removing material that is already there but no longer needed.

Many people hang on to, and live by, old fears and limiting beliefs that stand in their way and tell them what's *not* possible. But they need to let go of these blocks in order to live intuitively. The wonderful truths that lie in the superconscious cannot pass through such barriers of negativity.

In order to clean out subconscious obstacles, you need to bring them to consciousness, confront them squarely and honestly, and release them—let them go.

One way to do this is by working with your dreams. In *Lucid Dreaming,* Stephen LaBerge says that dreamwork can help you overcome anxieties, resolve inner conflicts and learn to accept inner parts of your-self—however nightmarish they may be.[2]

For instance, during a very vivid and lucid dream, a thirty-one-year-old woman watched herself age while sitting in her favorite rocking chair. First her blonde hair turned gray. Then her face wrinkled. Her body grew thin and gaunt. Suddenly, her hair and skin fell off and flew away, until only her skeleton was left. Then her bones, too, broke apart and flew off into a cloud of bright light. The woman felt no fear during the dream; indeed, at the end, she felt pleasantly warmed by the loving light into which her body had dissolved.

On waking and recalling the dream, the woman realized that she had previously been terrified of dying. But in that dream, she had released that fear. Now she could approach both dying—and living—with a new confidence and fearless enthusiasm.

As you progress along your intuitive path, sometimes you'll get stuck. You may need outside help in identifying and releasing obstacles to your growth. At such times, you could benefit from the guidance of a counselor, friend, support group, traditional therapist, or skilled channel.

One troubled woman, for example, sought intuitive assistance and advice to help rid herself of the intense guilt she'd been carrying around since she was molested as a child. The channel told the woman her guilt resulted from holding on to this painful past experience. "The only way to be released from the past," the channel said, "is through your own efforts to forgive your offender and yourself, so you can identify solely with the present."

The channel suggested that while meditating, the woman place her hands on her womb and contemplate the hurt she had felt there, physically and mentally—how being molested had seemingly damaged her personal strength and feminity. Then she told her to visualize releasing those feelings by throwing them into a fire. The channel further recommended that, following meditation, she undertake some physical action that would complete this cleansing process and make it real, such as painting a picture or performing a symbolic dance.

The cleansing process can sometimes be difficult, but it is the essence of spiritual growth. Channel Richard Lavin recalls that to get to his own truth, he had to go dig through a lot of old beliefs, ideas, and attitudes. "The intuitive exploration can be a painful journey," he admits realistically. "But on the other side of the pain is a grand sense of newness, of exuberance, of knowing your true self."

IMPROVE YOUR INTUITIVE RECEPTION

"By calming everyday thoughts," says the entity John through Kevin Ryerson, "ye can open what the mind truly is—a receiver to other forms of thought."

The key qualities required for the development of intuition are receptivity, acceptance, and sensitivity. In order to foster these qualities, improve your reception, and promote your intuitive progress, you need to calm your conscious mind.

Now, calming the conscious mind may sound like a simple thing to do, but silencing this erratic chatterbox is not necessarily so easy. Constantly racing with thoughts and concerns about myriad issues and events in your life, the conscious mind resists being stilled. But only when it is quiet, only when it releases its everyday attachments, will the superconscious be able to come through.

Calming the conscious mind can be aided through various forms of physical and mental relaxation, which include preparing the body through diet, exercise, breathing, meditation in one of its many forms, and the practice of various spiritual exercises to enliven and balance energy centers of the body in response to mental states. (Serious students of intuition will find suggestions for additional reading at the end of this book.) But, primarily, a calm conscious mind begins with a relaxed body.

You must learn to relax—deeply and completely. Two of the easiest exercises for deep relaxation come from one of the oldest spiritual disciplines—yoga. The first yoga exercise involves rhythmic breathing, and the second, a sequential relaxation of your body parts.[3]

To prepare for these exercises, wear unrestrictive clothing and select a quiet location. Choose a position, preferably seated with your spine erect and your feet on the ground. It should be comfortable enough for you to relax but not so comfortable that it encourages you to fall asleep.

Close your eyes and listen to your breathing. Concentrate on its steady rhythm: in and out, in and out.

Relax your body systematically by concentrating on each part, one at a time, moving from your toes up to your head. Let all tension flow out of each part, each bone, each muscle, until it relaxes completely. Travel upward, gradually continuing this process, until your entire body is deeply relaxed. You may want to go back a second time and check for any tensions you might have missed.

Once you have learned how to relax completely and calm your conscious mind, you will be ready to practice meditation, the most important tool for intuitive development and learning to channel.

MEDITATION: OPENING THE CHANNEL

Meditation is a mental process that carries the calm mind to an ultimate state of "nonthinking" and receptivity through developed mind control. The mental discipline necessary for meditation is often achieved by learning to concentrate your attention on a single focus, and then letting go of that focus.

One of humanity's oldest spiritual disciplines, meditation has assumed different forms and names in various religions and cultures throughout the centuries. You can find many instructive books and classes available on meditation techniques. Select the one that feels most suitable to you.

As you practice meditation, your intuitive faculties will develop and strengthen. You will experience increasingly heightened states of awareness. With determination and dedication, you will reach a state in which, says John White in *New Realities* magazine, "the ordinary sense of 'I'—the ego—is diminished while a larger sense of self-existence-merged-with-the-cosmos comes into awareness."[4] At that point of awareness, you can tap the universal reservoir of knowledge and channel intuitive information.

The intuitive process at this stage may manifest in different ways in different people. Some may feel the presence of a guide or a discarnate entity. Some may simply sense a higher level of themselves.

Some people may start communicating intuitive information through light-trance channeling and others through deep-trance channeling. (For in-depth descriptions of these channeling modes, see chapter 2.) Some nonverbal people may choose to express their intuitive insights through music, art, or healing work.

No one mode of channeling is "better" than another. As you're developing your own intuitive ability, don't precondition yourself to any particular mode. Instead, be open and receptive to how intuition best manifests in you.

INTUITIVE GROWTH IS AN INDIVIDUAL EXPERIENCE

For some, the development of intuition will be a short sojourn. For others, it may mean a lifelong journey. And as diverse as the time it takes, the experience itself will vary with each individual. "The core of the intuitive experience is common to all," says channel

Penney Peirce, who conducts "clarity and intuition training" seminars, "but not the form."

Initially, intuitive information reaches people in three ways—through the major sense preferences:

1. SIGHT. Intuition often communicates in a visual way, as do dreams. You may receive information in visions, images, symbols, or pictures. Some may be very realistic and others more abstract. As with dreams, you'll have to learn to interpret your symbols, to pull the truth from what comes through. This will require practice and you'll probably make some mistakes along the way. One developing channel, for instance, saw a symbol of Texas and told a friend he would move there. He didn't, but he did take a new job with a firm whose Texas Instruments computers bore the symbol of the state that she had described.

Don't get discouraged by misinterpretations. With experience, your accuracy will improve.

2. HEARING. A "voice" may deliver intuitive messages to you. It may sound like your own familiar voice. Or it may sound like someone else speaking to you inside your head or in a space around you.

Channel Sylvia Brown claims that when she was eight years old, a voice in her right ear spoke gently, "Dear Sylvia, don't be afraid. I come from God." She shrieked with fright until her grandmother explained that the voice was a benevolent "spirit," like a guardian angel, here to help her.

So don't be alarmed if intuition assumes an auditory form for you. Listen carefully and test what you hear.

3. TOUCH. Intuitive impressions may manifest themselves in your physical body. You may "feel" vibrations or sensations.

"Intuition doesn't only come into the mind," says Peirce. "Direct knowing can come through and be felt as impressions in your body. And if you extend that sensitivity farther, you can start feeling the energy field around you."

Pay attention to how your body feels—even when you're not meditating. Peirce recommends taking regular "body checks" throughout each day. Scan your body and see where it is holding tension, for example, and ask yourself why. Then you'll begin to understand how your body communicates intuitively with you.

As you progress along your spiritual journey, one means of accessing intuition may be more dominant than another, depending on your tendencies or skills. One person may be more visual. Another may relate better to sound. You don't need to worry about the means in which you're receiving information. Each person has his or her particular mode that is right for that person at the time. Eventually, if you work with one mode long enough, you may expand into others. You may evolve through many forms, perhaps starting off visually, progressing through hearing, then through feeling, to instantaneous direct knowing.

Basic Steps to Channeling

1. *Relax the body.* Tune into your rhythmic cycles, such as breath and heartbeat. Create a feeling of absolute safety within yourself. Quiet the conscious mind by moving down underneath the level of habitual chatter into peaceful silence. Center yourself inside your body. You may also scan the body from toes to head, relaxing all the parts systematically.

2. *Become aware of feelings and sensations.* Let go of any stressful emotions. Simply allow yourself to be sensitive to any impressions that may come to you.

3. *Alignment.* Acknowledge that you are fully present in your body in the present moment. Identify yourself as the higher self. Visualize yourself as golden light, radiating from every cell. Next move to the base of your spine and ground yourself to the center of the earth. Let pure energy circulate through your body from the earth and from your own being, raising the frequency level of your cells. Move to your heart center and breathe with a sense of connectedness and oneness with "all-that-is."

4. *Attunement.* Affirm your own true identity with such statements as "Be still, know that I am God"; "I am a pure source of love and wisdom"; "The spirit of truth (or the spirit of grace) lives within me"; and "The answers that are appropriate for me, and that serve my growth, already lie within me." Hold these thoughts and know that even higher levels of consciousness can channel through you. Be at peace.

5. *Focus on your need.* Picture your intended result, be it something physical or simply a feeling of completion. Feel the incompletion—the desire or curiosity.

Note: For deep-trance channels, who are completely unconscious during channeling, steps 6 through 9 need to be conducted by an assistant.

6. *Ask.* Activate the answer with 100 percent conviction. Make sure you state your request accurately and know what it is you are asking for.

7. *Release.* Pose the request to your higher self or guide. Have no doubts. Be in a state of perfect peace and trust. Wait in soft receptivity.

8. *Allow the inflow.* Make no judgments about what you receive, do no second-guessing, no refining with your conscious mind.

9. *Grant recognition.* Consciously recognize the answer in whatever form it takes—be it an inner image, voice or sensation, or an omen in outer reality.

10. *Record the answer.* Make the answer real for your body. Speak it, write it down or draw it.

11. *Express gratitude.* Give thanks to the various levels of yourself for cooperating with each other or to your guide. This validates the channeling experience.

12. *Implementation.* Follow through on what you get. Use the information. This completes the channeling experience.

Source: Penney Peirce, Clarity and Intuition Training, copyright © 1987. Reprinted with permission.

PROCEED AT YOUR OWN PACE

Intuition can manifest itself in a variety of ways, channeling being only one of them. As you develop new levels of consciousness, you may experience various paranormal phenomena such as astral travel or trance channeling. It is best to be open to whatever intuitive form is the most natural for you—at the proper time.

Don't jump ahead of your own natural progress, or you may pay a severe price. For instance, forcing yourself to trance channel prematurely—before you have learned the necessary lessons—could result in mental disturbance. It takes time to learn how to channel. The conscious and subconscious minds need to be properly prepared to conduct the flow of knowledge from the superconscious.

So if you feel the desire to astral travel or trance channel, make sure your own personal life path for spiritual development has reached the point where that is appropriate for you. It is best, and safest, if you pursue such phenomena as by-products of overall intuitive development and open up gradually to inner knowing.

REMEMBER TO BALANCE YOUR MENTAL SCALES

As you begin to refine your intuitive reception, confusing information, even garbage, may come to you. After all, abstract information from the superconscious mind must first travel through the subconscious mind, where it is translated into symbolic messages. Then the conscious mind converts those symbols into words or pictures that can be communicated to others. This is a complex process and requires practice as channels learn to be good interpreters who can clearly and accurately communicate intuitive knowledge.

So pay attention to whatever information you get. Play with it. Be like a child, not yet intuitively stifled, who has no fear of throwing out wild ideas or words that "don't make sense." For that's how you will progress to each next step that takes you closer to universal knowledge.

But don't forget to maintain a balance of intuition and logical thinking. Remember that intuition is a holistic *bridging* of the conscious and superconscious minds. You may be setting the rational mind aside, but you're not throwing it out. You're simply putting it in its proper place where it can coexist like a brother or sister with the intuitive part of your mind.

Test and evaluate the information you receive intuitively. Use the criteria in chapter 7 for determining the accuracy, credibility, completeness, and relevance of what you receive. Apply the same objectivity to your intuitive insights as you would to a skilled channel's.

As you begin to tap your intuition, a wealth of new knowledge will open to you. You'll realize that you were already being intuitive about lots of things, but you didn't acknowledge it. Your creativity and decision-making skills will improve. You'll find new, more meaningful answers to everyday concerns, as well as to broader humanitarian questions.

Your personal insight will grow too. You'll understand your own motivations better—why you do what you do. You'll discover more and more about who you really are and what your life is truly all about. You'll perceive your relationships with other people with new sensitivity.

You'll begin to align yourself with your life path, thereby speeding your spiritual growth. You'll learn how to create your own reality with new confidence and without so much struggle. You'll set new personal goals that reach higher than ever before.

And together with all the other people on the intuitive path, you will set in motion the New Age transformation to a richer and more humane society.

10. Catalyst for Widespread Change

Great men are they who see that spiritual is stronger than any material force, that thoughts rule the world.

RALPH WALDO EMERSON

Today, doctors are increasingly reconsidering their inadequate understanding of disease and recognizing what a influential role a patient's mind plays in causing and curing illness. Physicists, in the search for the nature of physical reality, are being confronted by fundamental paradoxes that sound more and more like metaphysical teachings from the Far East. Private consumers, even the materialistic so-called "yuppies," are investing in and purchasing products from companies that have socially responsible and humanitarian policies—forcing corporations to have a conscience. International boundaries are disintegrating as East meets West in multinational alliances, encouraging increased international travel and exciting cultural exchanges. Women, now a significant and powerful political force, are influencing changes in society that reflect their concerns for improved child care, more humane treatment of the aged, nuclear disarmament, and world peace. Individuals everywhere are starting to search internally for spiritual enlightenment and to work externally toward a "New Age" of social harmony.

At a time when the world teeters on the brink of an all-pervading transformation, people are looking for informational tools to prepare them for the New Age's scientific, cultural, and societal changes. Technology will surely assist this transformation, by offering new wonders of electronic wizardry to improve an individual's access to information and enhance global communication. But one of the most powerful tools for learning what is needed to assure planetary progress will be collective intuition.

As you have seen and perhaps experienced by now, intuition can be a potent resource for advancing personal growth. And as millions of people increase their individual awareness, the collective results of their raised consciousness will bear a major impact on tomorrow's society.

Already the United States, as well as other countries in the world, has felt a significant shift in values. Since the blossoming of the consciousness movement in the 1960s, success no longer equates automatically with the achievement of wealth and power at any cost. Materialism has begun to wane and is gradually giving up its priority position as people search for deeper meaning and higher quality in their lives. For many, that search eventually draws them into broader issues and more collective efforts to help humanity—such as holistic health care, improved educational systems, socially conscious corporate management, or political activism.

NEW AGE WELCOMES SIXTH SENSE

The New Age is dawning, and these value shifts are but a glimmer of changes yet to come. In the future, more people will heed and apply their intuition as this "sixth sense" becomes integrated into daily human functioning. Today's large grass-roots movement toward personal growth will continue as more individuals discover the value of intuition, and particularly channeled information, in their personal lives and in their work.

The numbers of skilled channels will multiply as intuitive counseling becomes a more accepted and respected profession. Their work will achieve greater public credibility and acceptance, first on the individual level and then on the institutional level.

Intuition has already made its way into the corporate boardroom on both the individual and group levels. Although still not the norm, greater numbers of executives and professionals are seeking intuitive counsel on personal and business matters. Occasional reports are increasing that Wall Street investors are turning to psychics for stock market guidance. Throughout the Western world, companies are sponsoring seminars on the development of intuition that promise to boost creativity and productivity. Bastions of higher learning, such as Stanford University, are integrating intuition courses into their management curricula. The "sixth sense" is permeating the world of institutions, and will continue to do so.

Progress toward full public acceptance of intuition as as a practical and reliable information source will certainly be slower for the more traditional public (governmental) organizations and the logic-entrenched scientific community. But eventually, as people everywhere begin to recognize intuition as a valuable and unlimited resource, it will earn its rightful place beside rational means of generating knowledge.

The integration of these two methods of knowledge generation—objective and subjective—working in cooperation with one another, can aid and greatly accelerate planetary progress. In what follows you will find two exciting examples of how intuitive resources, applied collectively, can generate otherwise inaccessible information and help humanity. Both approaches, "intuitive consensus" and "group attunement," demonstrate the distinct ways in which intuitive teams are already beginning to affect problem solving and decision making in today's society.

INTUITIVE CONSENSUS

The first approach, called *intuitive consensus,* uses teams of highly skilled channels, or expert intuitives, (independently interviewed) to generate solutions to unsolved problems facing science and society. This novel method of inquiry was developed over the past fifteen years by scientist William Kautz, who was frustrated with traditional, extremely lengthy, research methods.

Scientific research is mainly conducted by wrestling information from nature. To grow new knowledge, science relies upon a lengthy spiral of experimentation, observation, deduction, hypothesizing, more experimentation, and so on. The majority of the effort—as much as 80 percent in most areas of science—is spent searching for information to form hypotheses; the other 20 percent is spent validating correct hypotheses. The "search" eats up an enormous amount of time and effort.

But skilled channels can access new knowledge with clarity and accuracy in a matter of hours. Their intuitive resources can alleviate the critical but arduous searching part of the scientific process.

Intuitive consensus develops hypotheses based on detailed information solicited from teams of channels. This information is then available for validation according to traditional empirical methods, so that it can be communicated to the scientific world with credibility and can be accepted as part of scientific knowledge.

Here's how intuitive consensus works: First, for each topic of inquiry, a set of questions is very carefully prepared, to eliminate all bias and presumptions and to focus on the specific knowledge being sought. Second, these questions are posed *independently* to each member of a team of three or more channels (usually five). Each channel has been screened and qualified for demonstrated intuitive skill on both scientific and personal material. Finally, corresponding answers are compared with each other, as well as with existing knowledge, to form a coherent consensus of intuitively derived information. If significant ambiguities or actual differences are found among the various accounts (rarely the case), the cycle may be repeated on those questionable issues until clear hypotheses emerge. This body of information is then ready for scientific validation. At this stage, unforeseen ideas and new perspectives on problems frequently emerge, which can generate entirely new approaches.

Intuitively assisted research projects have been conducted at the Center for Applied Intuition and elsewhere in many areas including linguistics, archaeology, and anthropology. Over the past hundred years, for example, there have been a number of impressive and verified instances in which information from individual channels was crucial to the success of archaeological digs.

In 1908, Frederick Bligh Bond, director of excavations for the old ruined abbey at Glastonbury, England, sought the aid of channel John Bartlett. Through Bartlett's "automatic writing" ability, Bond established dialog with a long-deceased medieval monk who precisely directed Bond's unearthing of a large chapel and reconstruction of a totally destroyed shrine.[1]

In 1941, famous Polish psychic Stefan Ossowiecki, a chemical engineer by trade, took part in an experiment. Holding an artifact in hand, he described people and scenes from a Magdalenian culture that was 15,000 years old. His psychic descriptions were confirmed through archaeological analysis.[2]

And in 1971, Jeffrey Goodman, an archaeology graduate student at the time, was inspired by his own precognitive dreams to seek advice from Aron Abrahamsen, a Scandinavian channel living in Oregon. Abrahamsen's readings identified a specific, unsuspected site in Flagstaff, Arizona, and described what Goodman would find there. Over the next few years, Goodman excavated artifacts of early human beings from that site that astounded archaeologists.[3]

In each of these cases, impressive discoveries resulted from following the astoundingly accurate advice of individual channels. Intuitive consensus takes even further advantage of such valuable intuitive resources.

Intuitive consensus is the first research method to use *teams* of skilled channels. The team approach to the intuitive process has several advantages. It assures increased accuracy by automatically screening out the "coloring" that sometimes occurs as intuitive information passes through the channel's subconscious mind. It allows small errors or ambiguities that sometimes arise during the channeling process to be averaged out.

The team approach also stimulates the flow of information from channels by removing some of the pressure to perform perfectly, which they typically feel if they are sole consultants on an inquiry. It permits helpful feedback that can improve their performance. Finally, it creates a more comprehensive picture of the inquiry topic than would be presented by an individual channel.

Archaeological work has been conducted consensually by the Mobius Group in Los Angeles, using a staff of intuitive consultants.

And several intuitive consensus projects, covering a wide range of topics, have been successfully conducted at the Center for Applied Intuition. Channels have provided highly specialized and enlightening information regarding these worthwhile scientific and societal pursuits:

- How earthquakes are triggered
- The cause of sudden infant death syndrome (SIDS)
- The physiology and psychology of human conception, pregnancy, and childbirth
- The cause and treatment of manic depression

- The recreation of certain periods of ancient history
- A vision for elementary education for the twenty-first century
- The creative process
- Pyramid energy
- Optimum environmental conditions for psychic functioning
- The future of Japan

The results of some of these studies have startled even the most cynical skeptics of applied intuition.

In the late 1970s, intuitive inquiry into the baffling SIDS revealed both physiological and nonphysiological processes responsible for the disease. Several credible and verifiable hypotheses emerged. Although the Center for Applied Intuition was unable to check out the major hypotheses, incidental research reports from medical laboratories (who knew nothing of the intuitive inquiry) later substantiated two of the physiological explanations given by the intuitive team.

Thyroid abnormality shortly before death and neural brainstem anomalies in early infancy, both cited in the intuitive inquiry, were confirmed in studies reported by the University of Maryland School of Medicine and the Cleveland Medical Clinic, respectively. In addition, the frequent association of SIDS with poor family dynamics and poor prenatal nutrition was supported by an epidemiological study conducted independently the following year.

Intuitive consensus contributed these and other hypotheses regarding the causes of SIDS in only a few hours of work. Validation of these hypotheses would not be difficult by modern scientific methods. But conventional research would typically require years of work, simply to generate such credible hypotheses.

Parts of another intuitive consensus project, one dear to the hearts of Californians, have also been scientifically validated. "What triggers earthquakes?" was the query posed this time to a team of intuitives. In response, they agreed on a complex geophysical scenario (too intricate to describe here) involving an interaction of physical, chemical, and electrical forces in the atmosphere and the earth.

Two portions of this hypothesis appeared to be amenable to verification by conventional science. Funding was obtained from the U.S. Geological Survey (based upon nonpsychic arguments), and the projects were carried out at SRI International (where Kautz worked) from 1979 to 1983.

The first project studied unusual animal behavior, which the channels claimed was a valid precursor of earthquakes, not merely the supposed myth. A network of 1,500 volunteer observers of pets, farm animals, zoo animals and others—eventually, seventy species—were organized in seismic areas throughout California. The observers followed an established protocol and reported unusual animal behavior immediately on a telephone "hot line." A sophisticated statistical model analyzed the report data and earthquake data collected during the four-year life of the project. It was a quiet period for earthquakes in populated areas of California, but positive results were obtained from seven shocks.

In the second project, conducted independently by another SRI laboratory, electric field activity in the atmosphere was measured at a site near Hollister, California, deemed likely to experience small earthquakes. Records obtained from the two earthquakes closest to the measurement site showed marked variations in the atmospheric electric field during the quarter of an hour before the earthquakes—as predicted. Although not completely conclusive, it was a good start.

Some other aspects of the earthquake hypothesis were validated by returns to early records of earthquake effects: lights and chemical disturbances in the atmosphere just before or during earthquakes; electromagnetic effects; and the appearance of holes in the ionosphere (the protective electronic sheath above the earth's atmosphere) just before certain large earthquakes.

These scientific studies of only two aspects of the intuitively derived earthquake scenario cost nearly $300,000. Although that may seem expensive, it is actually cheap for scientific validation. Moreover, if the hypotheses had been generated by conventional cut-and-try methods, the cost would have been many times greater.

With the balance of this particular intuitive consensus project untested, there still exists a very credible theory to explain earthquake triggering. It doesn't contradict the contemporary scientific picture of the earthquake-triggering process (such as it is) as much as it goes beyond it—into the atmosphere, mainly, which geophysicists have not yet explored. With some aspects well-validated, the whole hypothesis certainly deserves to be tested. If proven correct, it could save tens or hundreds of millions of research dollars and many years of effort to create a practical earthquake prediction system.

THE FUTURE: FERTILE GROUND FOR INTUITIVE CONSENSUS

In all the studies generated by intuitive consensus, the information obtained has extended and complemented, rather than contradicted, already existing knowledge. Some inquiries have been completed and documented. But the scientific community has not yet opened its arms to applied intuition. So many inquiries are still sitting on shelves at the Center for Applied Intuition, waiting for forward-thinking sponsors to carry out the necessary testing and application. The future will surely bring forth these sponsors as scientists and research managers begin to recognize the limitless possibilities for using intuitive consensus to short-cut traditional, laborious efforts to grow new knowledge.

Consider how many factions of today's world are impeded by limited knowledge. People live in a confused or frustrated state of existence because they don't understand the meaning behind their trials and tribulations. Institutions operate at far less than optimal levels of efficiency and productivity because they lack information—in technology, economics, and human behavior. Science faces stone walls that hinder progress because it is so tedious to obtain needed information by strictly analytical means.

Think of all the effort that goes into obtaining information every day throughout society—for medical diagnosis, police investigations, legal cases, oil and mineral exploration, archaeology, financial predictions—you name it.

The skillful application of intuition could advance all of these causes. Intuitive consensus is particularly advantageous in areas of inquiry where progress is limited by lack of detailed knowledge or information, and where opportunities already exist for readily validating the proposed explanations. Some of the richest application areas are chemistry, physics, biology, economics, history, medical science and psychology, along with associated application fields such as engineering, business, law, health, and psychotherapy.

Ponder the impact intuitive consensus could have

on science and technology in such humanitarian efforts
as

- Identifying drugs for preventing or curing specific diseases or mitigating their symptoms
- Fabricating materials to have specific physical, biological and chemical properties; for example, alloys, ceramics, bioactive reagents, superconductors, grains, and special solvents
- Locating subterranean or submarine mineral deposits or buried objects
- Forecasting earthquakes, climatic changes, meteor falls, epidemics, and so on
- Understanding biological sensitivities; for example, identifying the particular organ with which birds sense magnetic fields, how dolphins communicate with one another, and how human sensitivities reach beyond the alleged limits of their sense organs.

And consider the contribution applied intuition could make to the business world in such efforts as inventing new products, identifying new markets, hiring human resources, predicting economic trends, solving organizational problems, and planning corporate strategies.

GROUP ATTUNEMENT

Group attunement is a second powerful way of using collective intuition. When a number of people, ranging from a few individuals to a large team, *collectively* apply their individual intuition in the proper way, they can generate rich new information that benefits the group. In this way, each individual acts as a channel for his or her partial contribution to the whole.

When applied to creative planning and decision making, group attunement allows all participants to play a valued and equal role. As each decision is made through this kind of shared involvement, no individual is the sole authority for new ideas or for answers. Moreover, the source of the answer is acknowledged as arising from a higher, uncontaminated level, rather than one member's personality or belief structure.

Several conditions are necessary for group attunement to work:

- A commitment to and trust in the process must be shared by all participants.
- An effective method of moving through individuals' personalities, beliefs, and feelings must be available; attunement needs a clear space in which to work.
- The questions posed must be clear and well defined.

Many forms and variations of group attunement are being practiced by communities and organizations throughout the United States and the world. For example, group attunement is being applied to the resolution of conflicts in personal relationships; to brainstorming among creative teams; and to decision making for working teams, clubs, committees, governing boards, organizations, and social communities.

Some entrepreneurial companies are looking to group attunement or similar processes to help them develop new, less bureacratic, organizational structures. Teams of managers and professionals, in small and large companies, are creatively using collective intuition to generate product ideas, apprehend systems, and identify market patterns.

Findhorn, a residential community in Scotland with about two hundred residents from many different countries, actively applies the group attunement process to its operation and government. Community members at Findhorn discuss facts and issues, express their feelings about them, and then participate in group meditation to obtain intuitive guidance. They share their experiences, assembling divergent views into a workable consensus that is good for the whole group. Findhorn members view attunement as a "step beyond democracy, a higher turn of the spiral in human attempts at self-government."[4]

INTUITION'S FAR-REACHING IMPACT ON SOCIETY

Frances Vaughan points out that the ancient Greeks considered intuitive knowledge to be the highest form of truth. As individuals open themselves up to inner knowing, the truth will indeed set them free.

And as the effectiveness of intuitive insight is experienced by more and more groups, organizations, and communities, its power as an information tool for planetary progress will become increasingly apparent.

Visualize some possible long-term effects on the way our social institutions might incorporate collective intuition in the future:

- Teams of expert intuitives will work together with scientists, executives and other professionals to greatly accelerate the resolution of major world problems.
- Intuitive consensus will become an accepted mode of group decision making on the committee, community, corporate, and global levels.
- Education in colleges, universities, and professional institutions will be extended so that intuitive resources are developed and implemented side by side with conventional, rational instruction.
- Collections (data bases) of specialized, intuitively derived information will be consulted via computer networks, and may eventually be integrated into libraries and publicly available data banks.
- Respect for and acknowledgment of the value of the intuitive process will spread among the public at large and then into government, industry, and other social institutions.

You can surely imagine many more, equally worthwhile applications of intuition for the future. Keep musing—your positive thoughts can promote a more promising tomorrow.

Vision of the Future:
Forecast by Kevin Ryerson

The future enters into us, in order to transform itself in us, long before it happens.

RAINER MARIA RILKE

The following forecast is a compilation of predictions from the discarnate entity "John," delivered through deep-trance channel Kevin Ryerson. The dates given are projected forward from the year 1987.

THE FUTURE IS YOU

Ye are beings that consist of mind, body and spirit. The spirit is the light, the mind is the builder, and the physical is the result. In your birth, ye have chosen to come into the earth plane to learn of your own celestial nature. For ye are not merely a physical body, but indeed, ye are a spiritual energy.

Ye would find that the spirit, or your superconscious mind, is a vast ocean of cosmic consciousness with which ye all are one. When ye incarnate, when this consciousness focuses itself through the physical body and ye are given birth, ye express the sum total of your past lives and all your future potentials.

How grand then, that ye are a human being of

mind and body? And how much grander when ye accept yourself as an immortal spirit?

Then the mundaneness of your life is transformed. Then ye can transcend all time and space. Then ye can live life no longer from a perspective that ye are a physical body that accumulates experience and dies, but instead, that ye are a spirit that is continuously conscious and ever-growing from one lifetime to the next.

Ye have chosen to wrap yourself in the flesh, so that ye may live life abundantly with each other. Sometimes, ye will have joy. Othertimes, ye will be heavy in your burden, feeling as though ye have passed the same way many times. Yet as your life spirals gracefully and gently upward, ye will ascend the circular path on which ye all are equal children of God.

As ye come and enjoin in the common spirit that is God, then ye become elements of the very vehicle of prophecy itself.

All prophecy extends from God. As one mind has many thoughts, so in turn the one God has many souls. And each of ye are indeed the souls of prophecy.

The manifestation of prophecy is merely the actualization of self. As ye think it is. In your heart so in turn are ye. Ye are that future that ye speculate upon.

But why look into the future or into the past, when ye should moreso look into the now—to that which ye are, to that which ye are manifesting? Why do ye desire to unfold the future? Do ye desire to manifest the future from a state of fear? Do ye desire to manifest the future from a state of speculation?

Or do ye manifest the future with a firm faith that is undoubting and ever rekindled in the natural expression of self? It is with this positive objective that we take a vision into the future to inspire your imagination and explore dimensions to come.

POLITICS FOR THE PEOPLE

Ye shall see continuing developments in political systems that will overhaul your democratic process, such as radical advances in electronic communications.

By the close of 1989, Sweden shall embrace the use of socialist forces or theory through electronic and computer technologies. Collective input from the general populace shall set a public or social agenda by priority votes and balloting. Then the citizens, whose names and other accords have been electronically encoded, shall vote on the general city agendas. This eventually shall eliminate an entire strata of government known as the legislature. For direct democratic principle shall amend the charter of events and the populace itself shall actually become the legislature. The executive branches of government shall merely set the agenda to be placed before popular vote. Each person shall become his or her own representative.

This shall result from developments in your telecommunications systems. More superior systems as well as universal electronic access to popular information systems shall enter and be socialized in the public domain.

This shall lead to the final unification of the ten nations in Europe. There may not be a "formal" bond between those nations as one governed political entity. But their economic and social forces shall be so interwoven that the advancement or retardation of any one particular country shall be instantaneously felt by all. It shall begin to be a model of political unification.

SPACE EXPLORATION

The first industrial base in space in a permanent or fixed orbit shall be explored within approximately three to seven years. It shall use minerals mined from the surface of the moon. This effort shall come out of a private economic interest represented by the Soviet Union, Canada, private innovative United States interests, and Australia.

ECONOMIC AND INDUSTRIAL TRENDS

Ye shall see new economic and industrial patterns developing in the United States over the next seven years. The national debt shall be refinanced. Outer extremes of interest rates on which these debts were financed, currently ranging from 20 to 30 percent, shall be radically reduced to a margin of 3 to 6 percent. The Third World debt is already being refinanced in this manner.

Multinational corporations shall cease to render specific services. They shall seek to consolidate their position and base of influence as financial industries or financial networks to promote the growth of transitory, middle-level industries. These corporations have succeeded in acquiring "hard assets." Now they may lease them back to the private sector and public interests.

As long as these individual multinationals remain split amongst general geographic regions, and forced to compete with mid-level financial institutions that they have no way of suppressing, an economic balance can be achieved. So there needs to be no consolidation—and no enslavement to any one central collapse of the economic systems.

Each generation of your technology shall proceed so rapidly that the average life span of any economic entity or industry shall be seven years or less. This shall cause not great upheavals, but a natural transitory element that shall allow people to experience greater leisure time. Within ten years, the work week shall be reduced to twenty-five hours. This reduction shall allow for periods of retraining and greater participation in the semisocial yet highly private sectors.

PRISON REFORMATION

Your prison system shall be reformed, making it a more humane one, a place of rehabilitation as is its philosophical ideal. Prisons shall be placed in areas of greater isolation rather than in central urban centers and shall perhaps border three or four states. By placing them in vaster wasteland areas, they can actually become communities in themselves. These particular innovations shall come about as a cooperation between governors, such as conferences, possibly led by politician Jerry Brown, in three to five years.

THE RISE OF TALL CITIES

Prototypal cities shall begin to arise in seven years, along the fringes of nationally acquired lands. These prototypal cities shall not cause urban decay. But cities shall level off their populations and create more stable economic solutions for citizens' housing and agricultural needs.

Taxes shall cease to exist. Public ownership in the industries generated shall be the financial backbone of all community endeavors. The community shall not be owned by the economic or central private interest but shall participate within it as a whole. To a great degree, this shall allow individuals to practice and develop their own theories within the protection, guidelines and restraints of social and economic forces that serve the collective as a whole.

New architectural principles shall radically overhaul construction of these cities. City structures shall be built that can house and feed a collective of 10,000 to 25,000 citizens, occupying no more land than ten to twenty-five acres.

Such efficient land use shall be possible because the city structure shall be a gigantic geosphere. It shall be suspended above the earth on no more than four central columns made of thin strands of crystallized titanium and aluminum alloys produced in zero-gravity states.

These cities shall be able to generate their own atmospheres—not through the use of chemical phenomena, but through harnessing micro-ecologies. Electromagnetic fields within the geospheres shall allow citizens a mode of transportation not unlike antigravity. Individual households shall have spartan furnishings.

These architectural technologies shall be developed on a microlevel for enclosed or individual domiciles within five to seven years, and then for larger geospheres in twenty-five years or after the turn of the century.

Ye shall still use wood and lumber as housing materials, but ye shall move toward radical acceptance of the reconstitution of such products. Ye will find greater value in new tempered structures, not unlike particle board, that shall be created with polymers and fibers of a metallike nature. On a microlevel, they shall have the same strength as reinforced concrete. These materials shall enable greater preservation and more efficient use of organically flexible materials such as woods—and shall add to their strengths.

NEW COURSE FOR EDUCATION

Ye have passed through a point of bulge in the human populace—which ye have quaintly labeled "baby boom"—resulting in a rapid decrease in school enrollments. This shall cause economic pressure for the collapse of the public school system in the United States. Ye shall see a disinvestment of educators who are highly sympathetic to universal standards of education. These individuals shall form collectives to follow the economic forces toward privatization. They shall be encouraged by public support for privatization as a source of innovation. They shall then be able to experiment with models of "superlearning," not currently evolved in the public school system because of lack of funding.

The superlearning models are based on the idea that the childhood learning process takes place from the first point of conception, and the stimulus received by the fetus, until the seventh year.

But many seek to first stimulate left-brain faculties such as mathematics, reading, and vocal articulation.

This shall prove incorrect as a model of learning. Children may learn this way, but it shall prove to be an emotional retardant. Such results shall begin to be observed as that first generation (so taught) develops toward adulthood. Leaving adolescence there shall be a noticeable decline in their ability to integrate emotion and intellect.

It shall then be observed that when right-brain faculties such as concept skills, appreciation and application of color are stimulated first, it is more effective. For then after the seventh year, when the child is thoroughly centered and can conceive more rapidly, left-brain faculties such as mathematics, observation, symmetrical skills, and reading can be developed. In this way, children shall have the imagination to apply these more mundane tools because they shall have the ability to conceive their usefulness—versus having these tools forced upon them as part of an unidentified learning direction.

Since ye parents have authority over the development of your children during these first critical seven years, ye should study such advanced models as Waldorf, Montessori, and other superlearning models and apply them in the order suggested.

By the tenth to twelfth year, adolescents shall be able to achieve that which ye now consider second and third levels of college. Then after their twenty-first year, they shall be granted a complete period of sabbatical to fully integrate what they have learned before they begin a career. The sabbatical shall be considered critical to their development as wholly integrated and responsible adult personalities.

Then they shall progress within the social order according to their own pace and their own needs. Society shall no longer place unnecessary stress on individuals to achieve economically or socially before their years, because life spans shall eventually pass the century mark.

MEDICAL MARCH TOWARD HOLISTIC HEALING

The medical industry shall continue its trend toward holistic practices. Too many graduates in the medical sciences shall cause economic upheaval, forcing the industry to decentralize. Doctors shall open individual clinics specializing in holistic medicine in response to people seeking this form of treatment. Encouraged by documented biofeedback studies, the medical community shall come to accept nutrition, diet, and visualization as standard clinical techniques for treating disease.

Ye shall see nutrition being used as a major form of medicine within the next three to seven years. The former dietary patterns of parties such as Hopi and Navaho will be rediscovered. Ye shall also study people in well-preserved Chumash settlements, in regions around Carpenteria, California.

There shall be a shift from the heartlands of your country to the southern portions as your agricultural center. New nutritional elements shall be discovered from the desert floor and from local fauna. Dietary advances involving hybrid forms shall be made not through genetic engineering but through traditional cross-breeding.

Exploration into the sciences of altered states shall cause overhauls in medical treatments. For example, it is documented that individuals who enter into ecstatic or hypnotic states may recall psychotraumas and on command cause reappearances of welts or other blows suffered in childhood. Phenomena like these shall be explored under more controlled conditions—not through drug-induced states but through meditative, hypnotic, sound-induced, and light-induced altered states. Guided visualizations shall even be able to cause rejection of tissue foreign to the body, such as cancerous growth. These studies shall lead to new capacities to generate psycho-immunity and even result in "psychic surgery."

Psychic surgery—physiological surgery where no knife is used—shall be documented and practiced within seven to ten years. This shall come about by studying the fact that the mind may so carefully regulate not only individual blood flows, but even individual cell tissues. For example, skin or muscular tissue may be commanded to be folded back under strong hypnotic or altered states. These studies shall lead to the clinical practice of these forms of surgery.

Look for the applications of electromagnetic and electrical fluidiums to be applied to the healing states, in particular healing through the independent electrical system known as *meridians*. Better documentation of such applications shall come out of Sweden, Japan, China, New Zealand, Australia, Nigeria, and Brazil.

METAPHYSICAL BOOSTS FOR HUMAN PRODUCTIVITY

Telepathy, a way of penetrating deeply into the mind, shall be used as a psychological tool and eventually as a form of highly sophisticated communications for basic thought data within three to five years. There shall be individuals who may hold such a pure state of well-being and mind that it is transferable to others strictly through a symbionic or telepathic link. In the East, this is called "transference of spiritual presence."

Within nine years, color shall prove to have impact on physical well-being and consciousness. Telepathy and the phenomenon of the aura shall cause whole transformations in your society, increasing human productivity by 10 to 20 percent.

Light and color may become an issue between labor and management. Ye can project an environment through full-spectrum therapies of lighting regulated throughout the day. The effect of sunlight as a whole vibrant stimulant on the autonomic and sympathetic nervous system shall be studied. Physical anatomy and cellular levels can be stimulated by individual spectrums. Ye shall find many other health benefits as well.

Stress, of course, shall be discovered to be the major factor in blocking the development of intelligence. New insights into intuitive concepts or right-brain models shall result in new forms of "intelligent emotions" that shall be more accurate, more humane, and indeed of greater value in dealing with the phenomenon ye call "future shock."

Those with multiple disciplines and intuition based more on Japanese models and theories for advancements in life shall adapt better to the dynamics of future economic and job forces. Those with developed intuition and creativity shall adapt more easily to shorter industry life spans. Such individuals shall be able to make smooth transitions and look forward to multidimensional careers.

MOVING AROUND THE PLANET

Ye shall see these activities and trends within the overall pattern of earth changes:

The earth's axis, which has already shifted a full degree in the last 150 years, shall gradually shift as much as another two degrees over the next 30 to 40 years. This may eventually result in a shift of a full three to four degrees.

There shall be increase in rainfall throughout southwest desert regions, to such a degree that they shall eventually become semitropical.

There shall be increased volcanic activity throughout the Pacific Rim Basin and on the European continent within three years. Architectural advances that shall be sought in Japan, Mexico City, and Italy may greatly alleviate the human suffering caused by such activity. Ye shall find stability in New Mexico, the Pacific Northwest, Northern California and the Midwest in the United States, and in New Zealand, Australia, and the Hawaiian isle chain. Between the close of November, and projecting into the fourth or fifth day of December 1987, ye shall see some earthquake activity reaching 3 to 4 on the Richter scale in the center of the city of Los Angeles in the early morning hours. The earthquake shall cause more of a gentle rolling rather than a sharp jolt to the city. But the very fact that its epicenter is in the city shall cause increased concern, particularly regarding any tunneling activities beneath Los Angeles. This may delay development of an inner mass transit system based on electronics and rail systems.

India may be subjected to greater tidal activities. The coastline of California shall experience first tidal activities, then increased earthquake activity, but not until the latter close of the century. (And not even then, if ye place a seed of calmness in your mind now. Continue to hold it there and ye can institute that positive thought.)

A FAR GLIMPSE INTO THE FUTURE

Ye who merge the mind, the body and the spirit shall experience greater longevity; that is, literally, a longer life in the physical body. With longer life spans, ye shall have greater opportunity to work out karma. For it is said that if there is death, sin lies at the door. Sin simply means to have missed the mark. It simply means to have gone astray of the natural laws.

To be human is to be of mind, body and spirit. To be human is not simply to err, but to forgive the error, in that ye are spirit, and spirit transcends the error.

How can your mind enter into the threshold of the spirit? Through meditation.

Through meditation, comes discovery of the inner self. So meditate. Merge yourself with nature, with what is termed in the Orient as "the Tao," "the Way," the "inner light." Learn to make yourselves fully aware beings. For ye never slumber, ye never die. Your subconscious is active. How much moreso, then, the superconscious? Merge your subconscious, conscious, and superconscious. Merge yourself in mind, body, and spirit.

For if ye perceive life only through the five physical senses, then ye are indeed limited. For the five physical senses perceive height, width, depth, time, and space. But when mind expands into the perimeters of past lives, for example, ye are transformed. When the mind expands into future potentials, ye are transformed. Reality, in terms of the five physical senses, crumbles—not to die, but to be transformed into a new reality, a new society, a new humanity.

Your meditations, your deepening of consciousness, your deepening of love for each other, shall result in less strain and stress on the body. The body shall have greater immunity, greater assimilation of nutrients, and therefore increased longevity. And ye shall approach life spans from 125 to 150 years.

By the year 2,000, the average life span shall be between 80 and 100 years. By the year 2025, 125 years; by the year 2075, 200 years; by the year 3,000, ye shall have fulfilled the thousand years of brotherhood—physical immortality.

The physical body shall then be incorruptible, and shall return naturally to the earth from whence it has sprung forth. For in those days, ye shall draw up your bodies and consciously incarnate. Your consciousness shall embrace the whole of your lifetimes lived and, indeed, shall embrace the whole of your consciousness. And your sciences shall be psychic, of the mind and of the soul.

And then there shall be no nations. There shall be only one planet, one people. For there is only one race—the human race.

Appendix: A Directory of Channels

The following list of channels is offered as a exemplary resource for those who are seeking more information or other assistance, and who do not already have access to qualified channels. It is obviously not comprehensive; there are surely hundreds of channels in the United States alone, many of them very competent, who are not listed here.

The Center for Applied Intuition has classified these channels into three groups:

A. Those already qualified by CAI, which vouches for their integrity and the quality of their work as sources of personal guidance and accurate information.
B. Those that come highly recommended, but whom CAI has not adequately checked out.
C. Those who have come to CAI's attention, but about whom little or no relevant information is available.

Again, assignment to Groups B and C has more to do with CAI's opportunities to observe these channels than with their competence. All channels listed have given permission to include their names on this list, and in most cases have supplied their own descriptive paragraph (sometimes edited down by us).

GROUP A

Aron Abrahamsen
P.O. Box 5008
Everett, WA 98206

Aron, a graduate electrical engineer who worked in the aerospace industry for twenty years, is a trance channel. Aron and Doris, his wife, have been providing life readings and some research readings on a regular daily basis since 1970. The method used is deep meditation, leaving the body to go to the Akashic Records to obtain information. All the readings are done remotely—that is, without the client being present. He has completed more than twenty research readings with the Center for Applied Intuition.

Lenora Huett
470 Suncrest Way
Watsonville, CA 95076

Lenora has done psychic and spiritual counseling for clients in the United States and foreign countries for twenty-four years. Her counseling experiences include personal relationships, business, scientific research, spiritual guidance, past-life relationships and/or lessons, etc. Four books have been published from material channeled through her. She works from a question-answer format; the time and thought spent in preparation helps make the reading a more meaningful experience. Lenora has worked extensively in scientific readings with the Center for Applied Intuition.

Sanaya Roman
P.O. Box 19117
Oakland, CA 94619

Sanaya has been channeling Orin, a high master spirit teacher, for over ten years. She is an advisor to individuals, groups, and businesses. She is the author of the books *Living with Joy* and *Personal Power Through Awareness*. She teaches ongoing courses in channeling with Duane Packer, co-author with Sanaya of *Opening to Channel: How to Connect with your Guide*. Sanaya has produced over one hundred guided meditation tapes by Orin. (A free catalog of tapes, books, and classes is available by writing to the address above.)

Kevin Ryerson
3315 Sacramento Street #603
San Francisco, CA 94115

Kevin is a fully accredited trance channel in the tradition of Edgar Cayce and Jane Roberts. During the past fifteen years he has taught, lectured, and conducted seminars in the field of parapsychology and the intuitive arts. Well respected for his balanced and integrated world view, Kevin provides an experience that has touched many people. He has worked extensively with medical doctors, scientists, parapsychologists and other professionals, and is a major contributor to several books besides this one. Kevin has been a frequent guest on national television and radio. He figures prominently in Shirley Mac-Laine's best-selling books *Out on a Limb* and *Dancing in the Light,* and appeared in the TV miniseries based on the former book. He has worked extensively with the Center for Applied Intuition.

The following twelve channels are CAI staff readers, and may be contacted through

The Center for Applied Intuition
2046 Clement Street
San Francisco, CA 94121
(415)221-1280

Jon C. Fox

Jon is an electronics engineer whose interest in new energy devices led him to channeling as a source of new knowledge and principles. The energy being known as "Hilarion" that manifests through him in the trance state is especially concerned with awakening our human capacity for universal love, and often speaks of opening the heart. Hilarion also provides valuable and enlightening technical information useful to physicists, healers, astrologers, and others.

Joan S. Grigsby

Joan is a clairvoyant reader in private practice since 1973. She teaches meditation and metaphysics, specializing in translating "mystery school" training into present-day lifestyle. Her background is in psychology, philosophy, and business.

Richard Lavin

Richard has been involved in spiritual and metaphysical training for many years, studying Tai Chi, transcendental meditation, psychic awareness, and psychology, culminating in his studies as a certified hypnotherapist. He channels a personality "Ecton" who is able to address a wide range of topics, including past lives, health, diet, life direction, relationships, sexuality, and many others. Ecton is able to sift through superficialities and blockages and get to the root of understanding in a very personal and concise fashion. The channeled messages are rooted in concepts of unlimited creativity and mental power, personal responsibility, divine trust and guidance, and unconditional love and acceptance.

Lin David Martin

Lin has been personally involved with meditation and healing since 1961. His work as a trance channel and clairvoyant began in 1971 after an eight-year study with an American Indian spirit teacher. Lin works actively throughout America and Europe as teacher and reader, focusing on helping individuals better understand their own deepening nature, with specific emphasis on unfolding potentials of creativity, healing and intuition. The spiritual presence that speaks through Lin offers guidance with depth, precision, clarity, and compassion—and often a fine sense of humor!

Charles Nunn

Charles is a certified medium, Ro-Hun practitioner, hypnotherapist, and ordained minister. He combines his psychic and intuitive practice with twenty-two years experience in business administration and economics. His professional practice includes personal, group, institutional and corporate counseling, past-life regressions, visioning, lecturing, psychometry, and the investigation of psychic phenomena. Charles is motivated by a strong desire to assist individuals and groups in recognizing, accepting, and refining their own intuitive communications with the divine, creative force.

Suzann Owings

Suzann, whose doctorate is in futures research and organizational structures, uses her psychic abilities to help individuals and groups tap into their own intuitive wisdom and powers, and to harmonize the spiritual and material planes of their existence. The style of her readings is intimate and gentle, yet insightful and penetrating. Her clients often comment that she seems to become the voice of their own hearts and souls, and to speak the wisdom of their essence.

Penney Peirce

Penney is a gifted clairvoyant and intuition development trainer, working with both United States and Japanese clients.

She brings a unique combination of humor, practicality and inspiring insight to her spiritual counseling and teaching. She has studied spirituality cross-culturally and from many angles, and has been a sensitive and acute observer of human behavior. Penney's consultations are characterized by a clear and immediate focus on key pivotal issues and description of the subtleties of the personal growth process. In addition, she has worked for ten years as a corporate art director. This combination of skills gives her an unusual ability to communicate about the elusive nature of intuition in a practical way.

Mary Gillis Reins

Mary is a clairvoyant reader, teacher of metaphysics, children's teacher, fine arts painter, and healer, and has taught others to perform readings. With a foundation in mystical Christianity, Kriya Yoga, metaphysics, and the Course in Miracles, she endeavors to enhance the holiness in those she touches. She feels that right-mindedness consists of opening to our fullest capacity to love and respond to our inner voice. Mary's readings have been described as compassionate and precise. Her specialty and current work is in attitudinal health and healing.

Barbara Rollinson

Barbara Rollinson, M.S., is an accomplished deep-trance channel, and president of Rollinson and Associates, a metaphysical-educational center dedicated to world service through transpersonal growth, spiritual healing and the trance channeling process in an environment of love and support. Barbara telepathically channels dolphins, and is writing a book on that subject. She teaches the matriarchal medicine way, as well as a variety of other personal and spiritual growth techniques.

Nancy X. Sharpnack

Nancy X. Sharpnack, M.A., is a trance channel for the wise, gentle being Etherion. They conduct workshops together on a broad spectrum of issues ranging from personal creativity to New Age cosmology. Many claim Etherion's loving, validating approach has effected profound healings for them. A wide range of topics are covered in the life readings: enhancing intuition, spirit guides, career, relationships, health, letting go of fear, past lives, the inner child, and others. Etherion welcomes all questions.

Richard Wolinsky

Richard, who has a B.A. and M.A. in philosophy, is a deep-trance channel in the style of Jane Roberts, and was a regular member of her "Seth" class for two years. He is a writer, editor, and radio interviewer by profession. His focus is on the exploration of personal growth and consciousness, drawing on ideas and inspiration from the Seth Material. His entity Martenard is both challenging and loving. Richard provides personal readings and conducts personal group sessions in the San Francisco Bay Area, Los Angeles, and New York.

GROUP B

Michael Crumbacher
P.O. Box 1043
Larkspur, CA 94939

Michael has been involved with the channeling process for six years and currently channels three entities: Joseph, Jaas, and Blanch. His focus is the awakening of the spiritual being within those he comes into contact with, through personal consultation and small group sessions. Humor and a self-empowering love are the important elements of his channelings. He lives and works in Mill Valley, California.

Duane Packer

P.O. Box 19117
Oakland, CA 94619

Duane has been channeling a master entity named DaBen, who is bringing through a framework of thought around the body-mind-spirit and working with the energy fields of the body to align the life force into its highest pattern. He is currently writing/channeling several books (some with Sanaya Roman) and teaching courses for professionals on the body's energy patterns. Duane, a geophysicist by profession, has had a practice in body work for over eight years, ranging from deep-tissue work with sports and other injuries to energy balancing and psychic healing to personal empowerment growth programs. He is combining his extensive scientific knowledge with the ability to "see" energy, with the goal of empowering the individual.

Jach Pursel

c/o Concept: Synergy
P.O. Box 159 (N)
Fairfax, CA 94930

Jach Pursel has been channeling the entity Lazaris continuously since 1974, through private consultation, workshops, audio and visual tapes, and soon through several books. Lazaris's goal is to empower us: to give us the tools and understanding to create our own realities with the utmost effectiveness and joy, and to help us take back the power we so often have given away. Lazaris is there to show us how to allow ourselves the ultimate adventure: to rediscover how completely loved we are by God/Goddess/All That Is, and how deep is our own capacity to love.

Kathy Reardon
P.O. Box 880557
San Francisco, CA 94188-0557

Kathy Reardon is a trance channel through whom speak three spirits: Moira from fifteenth-century Ireland, Harganon from Andromeda, and Arkon from the Pleiades. The focus of her work is to help people become comfortable developing their own intuition. Her spirit guides provide individuals with a broader perspective on their lives by offering information with a unique blend of Irish wit and cosmic wisdom.

Judi West
P.O. Box 9837
Santa Fe, NM 87504

Drawing on her background in psychology, metaphysics, and business, Judi provides direct access to information for individuals and systems, accessing insights that accelerate growth, creative expression, problem solving, and discovery. She has worked since 1974 with clientele of a national and international referral network, drawn from medicine, administration, education and science, seeking assistance in spiritual, personal, and professional growth. Judi is author of two books: *The Brothers* and *Personal Growth Training Questionnaire and Handbook.*

Elissa Heyman
1111 Jones Street
San Francisco, CA 94109

Elissa is a psychic counselor and healer who has worked with people in San Francisco since 1979. Her training is in psychotherapy, psychic channeling and healing. She articulates clients' inner guidance, the healing procedures they will respond to, and answers to specific questions using channeling and tarot. She consults in person and by telephone, and conducts "healing circles" for individual and group healings. She also does psychic counseling and guided imagery visualizations on NBC radio.

Jean Moshofsky
229 Chenery
San Francisco, CA 94131

Jean's training began at Heartsong School in Berkeley, California, where she taught for six years and included study with Helen Palmer and others. She has worked as a clairvoyant consultant for eight years, using her ability in developing relationship, work, and problem-solving profiles for her clients. She is known for her extensive accuracy in almost all areas of questioning. She also teaches classes in clairvoyant development and inner transformation.

Joan Morton
2186 14th Avenue
San Francisco, CA 94116

Joan Morton's ability as a clairvoyant reader developed while she was in a convent following her nursing career. Her gift enables her to define and sort out emotional, spiritual and physical life issues. By putting them into perspective, she promotes understanding, resolution and healing. Her primary concern is your awareness of how much power *you* have over your life. Her hour-long readings are taped, in person or by telephone.

Allen Hicks
21 Enterprise Dr.
Corte Madera, CA 94925

Allen has been practicing clairvoyant readings since 1980, integrating his channeling work since 1985, and now functions as a deep-trance channel, focusing on personal readings. The entity for his channeling is a native American Indian guide, Tsamnisa, and attention is on major life issues—money, sex, and death—from the viewpoint that these issues serve as vehicles for the understanding of self. He has been a guest lecturer at the Center for Applied Intuition in San Francisco, and is currently on the Board of Directors of the Spiritual Sciences Institute in Santa Barbara.

B. Ann Rowan
1401 Slater St.
Santa Rosa, CA 95404

Ann Rowan, M.A. psychology, is a state-certified psychology instructor, lecturer, trainer, teacher, and student of meditation with sixteen years experience in parapsychology. She is presently serving a three-year appointment as a member of Sonoma County Advisory Board on Drug Abuse. She conducts training seminars and is devoted to bringing her New-Age knowledge and truths to the poor and less financially fortunate, through expanding their awareness and understanding of psychic potential.

Betty Bethards
Inner Light Foundation
P.O. Box 761
Novato, CA 94948

Betty Bethards is a widely known psychic, mystic, spiritual healer, and meditation teacher. Sometimes called "the common sense guru," she has helped millions in their search for self-understanding through the tools of dreams, visualizations, affirmations and meditation. She is the author of six books, including *Be Your Own Guru,* and is president of the nonprofit Inner Light Foundation, which sponsors monthly lectures, media appearances, and workshops with Betty.

Gabriele Blackburn
P.O. Box 246
Ojai, CA 93023

Gabriele works with people on health and psychology related problems: intuitive healing, laying on of hands, and visualization meditation healing. She shows people how to resolve their own situations and be in their own light. She has worked with the Phyllis Krystal method of "Cutting the Ties that Bind" for over twenty years. Gabriele is the author of the book *The Science and Art of the Pendulum,* and a cassette tape, *Protecting Yourself.* She is especially interested in working with those willing to go deeply into themselves to resolve the problems that plague them. Gabriele does not do readings solely for the purpose of giving information, but prefers to work in a variety of ways with each person to help them discover their own freedom.

Evelyn Glassmeyer
506 Goodman Road
Pacifica, CA 94044

Evelyn Glassmeyer, M.A., is a metacounselor whose unique practice includes channeled readings, counseling and therapy, and therapeutic body work in Pacifica, California. She channels the Council of Twelve to help people connect to their soul purpose, heal through imagery, and develop self-loving skills. Evelyn does long-distance readings, conducts day-long healing intensives, and teaches channeling in the San Francisco Bay Area and in Texas. She has long studied metaphysics, transpersonal therapies, and self-healing, and she has been a holistic therapist and channel for eight years.

GROUP C

Rev. Roberta S. Herzog
P.O. Box 808
Wyalusing, PA 18853

Roberta provides guidance through evidential access into the Akashic Records, following sixteen years experience with past-life readings and twenty-five years as a student and teacher of the Wisdom Teachings. She is spiritually trained with responsible ethics. A portion of her fee goes to charity. Each client receives a tape of the reading and a descriptive monograph on Akasha. Every courtesy is given. Thank you for the privilege of serving. Namaste.

Samuel Holland
16593 Ferris Ave.
Los Gatos, CA 95032

Samuel enters into a deep meditation, forming a consciousness where universal energies are tapped. In that atmosphere of love and compassion he channels information, and answers questions for individuals, groups, and corporations. Samuel's work has been helpful in crisis counseling as well as developing high-technology products for Silicon Valley companies. He is president of the Foundation for the Recovery of Ancient Wisdom, for which he lectures, teaches, and conducts psychic and physical archaeological research in many countries.

Dale S. Ironson, Ph.D.
245 West Blithedale Avenue
Mill Valley, CA 94941

Dale is a management consultant who specializes in giving presentations and training programs for corporations on how to develop and use intuition and creative channeling techniques in solving problems and enhancing the performance of sales, advertising, marketing, management, and research and development professionals. Dr. Ironson has served as a member of the Human Resources Department of Stanford University Medical Center, and as a columnist on creativity for *International Television* magazine. He is currently on the faculties of the Institute of Transpersonal Psychology, and the Graduate School of Consciousness Studies at John F. Kennedy University.

Virginia Essene
1556 Halford Avenue #288
Santa Clara, CA 95051

Using the Gold Ray energy (Christ Consciousness) in "powercell" partnership with the Silver Ray (through Ann Valentin), Virginia brings to humanity her cosmic lectures, seminars, and individual soul readings. These hour long readings clarify each soul's purpose and cancel prior negative imbalances if the purpose is completed. Through her seeking and spiritual service, she has channeled three recent books: *New Teachings for an Awakening Humanity, Secret Truths for Teens and Twenties,* and *Cosmic Revelation—Channeled Milestone of Truth.*

Sylvia C. Brown
Nirvana Foundation
3190 S. Bascom Avenue, Suite 200
San Jose, CA 95124

Sylvia, a full-time professional psychic since 1974, has appeared as a guest on many television and radio shows and has been the subject of (and has contributed to) several books and articles. Since 1982 Sylvia has taught courses in parapsychology at De Anza Community College. Sylvia founded the Nirvana Foundation for Psychic Research, a nonprofit organization dedicated to researching parapsychology. Her ongoing psychic work involves private appointments, lectures, and seminars. She counsels all who are in need.

Ann Valentin
1556 Halford Avenue #288
Santa Clara, CA 95051

Ann is a trance medium for the Silver Ray energy, twin souls of God's first creation. Silver Ray, creator of the rainbow and maker of our moonlight, is contacting the earth now to help each soul come forth to fulfill its purpose for peace. She works with copartner Virginia Essene in giving individual soul readings and group spiritual education seminars. Ann has just completed with Virginia a new book, *Cosmic Revelation.*

Kathryn Ridall
17604 Runnymede
Van Nuys, CA 91406

Kathryn Ridall, Ph.D, is trained in western psychology and the intuitive arts. She teaches channeling classes, has written several articles on channeling, and integrates channeling into her counseling work. She is currently running channeling support groups for people in the entertainment industry in Los Angeles.

Eric Teissedre
1750 Kala Kaua Ave. #3-834
Honolulu, Hawaii 96826

Eric, with a background in astrology, palmistry, and African and Indian spiritualism, has been involved with metaphysics and psychic work for twenty-four years. He is presently conducting weekly spiritual services in Hawaii and psychic counseling both in person and by mail. His readings consist of divinely inspired specific information in all aspects of life. He communicates with a individual's spiritual essence and channels a higher vibration to improve the karma and give guidance to the individual. Eric has an international clientele and has appeared on radio (on his own show), television and in a number of publications.

Dagmar Morrow
505 Cypress Point Drive #214
Mountain View, CA 94043

Dagmar Morrow is a highly trained psychic, healer, and medium. She does counseling, lectures, teaches, and writes articles on the use of intuition.

Judy Christenson
12763 Leander Dr.
Los Altos Hills, CA 94022

Judy, who has a doctorate in clinical psychology, channels teachings from higher consciousness, working with several entities. Her readings, focused more on evolutionary development than on day-to-day problem solving, follow a nontraditional metatherapy, a process developed through channeling that works through heart emotion rather than traditional belief emotion. She is teaching an ongoing weekly class for consciousness growth and change, and is developing a course to teach this process to other therapists.

Mark Wallek
7300 S.W. 86th Street
Portland, OR 97223

Mark is a professional psychic devoted entirely to advancing the concepts and practice of intuitive skills. His thirteen years of work has earned him an endorsement from *Reflections* magazine, Portland's holistic resource directory, for his "sensitive work, clear-eyed scholarship in esoteric psychology, and carefully teaching others." He has set a standard of honesty and usefulness and is the premier publically available psychic in the Portland area. He offers individual consultations, workshops, and classes.

Notes

Chapter 1

1. Christmas Humphreys, *Zen Buddhism* (New York: Macmillan, 1974), pp. 1, 108.
2. Marcia Moore and Mark Douglas, *Yoga: Science of the Self* (York Cliffs, Me.: Arcane Publications, 1967), pp. 86–89.
3. John J. Delaney, ed., *Saints for All Seasons* (Garden City, N.Y.: Doubleday, 1978), pp. 89–97.
4. Brewster Ghiselin, *The Creative Process* (New York: New American Library, 1952), pp. 45, 64, 180.
5. R. M. Hare, *Plato* (New York: Oxford University Press, 1982), pp. 20, 35.
6. Quoted in Marie-Louise von Franz, *C. G. Jung: His Myth in Our Time* (New York: Putnam's, 1975), pp. 49, 284.
7. Philip Goldberg, *The Intuitive Edge* (Los Angeles: Tarcher, 1983), p. 76.
8. Jeffrey Mishlove, *The Roots of Consciousness* (Berkeley: Random House and The Bookworks, 1975), p. 306.
9. Stuart Berg Flexner, *Listening to America* (New York: Simon & Schuster, 1982), p. 486
10. Flexner, p. 487.
11. Mishlove, p. 75.
12. Willis Harman and Howard Rheingold, *Higher Creativity: Liberating the Unconscious for Breakthrough Insights* (Los Angeles: Tarcher, 1984), p. 67.
13. Doris Agee and Hugh Lynn Cayce, ed., *Edgar Cayce on ESP* (New York: Warner Books, 1969), p. 8.
14. John Naisbitt, *Megatrends* (New York: Warner Books, 1982), p. 35.
15. John W. White, "What Is Meditation?" *New Realities* (September–October 1984), p. 51.
16. Marilyn Ferguson, *The Aquarian Conspiracy: Personal and Social*

Transformation in the 1980s (Los Angeles: Tarcher, 1980), pp. 23, 24.

17. Shirley MacLaine, *Out on a Limb* (New York: Bantam Books, 1983).

Chapter 2

1. Frances E. Vaughan, *Awakening Intuition* (Garden City, N.Y.: Doubleday, 1979), p. 3.
2. Ellen Armstrong, "Bottom-Line Intuition," *New Age Journal* (December 1985), p. 33.
3. Harman and Rheingold, p. 134.
4. Harman and Rheingold, p. 135.
5. Quoted in Von Franz, p. 124.
6. Quoted in Von Franz, p. 124.
7. Agee and Cayce, p. 37.
8. Meredith Lady Young, *Agartha: A Journey to the Stars* (Walpole, N.H.: Stillpoint, 1984), p. 41.
9. C. Q. Yarbro, *Messages from Michael* (New York: Berkley Books, 1980), pp. 21, 22.

Chapter 3

1. Hilarion and Maurice B. Cooke, *Threshold* (Toronto: Marcus Books, 1980), p. 5.
2. Meredith Lady Young, p. 309.
3. Joseph Head and S. L. Cranston, *Reincarnation in World Thought* (New York: Julian Press, 1969).
4. Head and Cranston, p. 8.
5. Head and Cranston, pp. 109–13.
6. Sylvia Cranston and Carey Williams, *Reincarnation: A New Horizon in Science, Religion and Society* (New York: Julian Press, 1984), p. 222.
7. Head and Cranston, pp. 269–80.
8. Head and Cranston, pp. 309, 310.
9. Henry Wadsworth Longfellow, *The Complete Poetical Works of Henry Wadsworth Longfellow.* Cambridge Edition (Boston: Houghton Mifflin, 1893), p. 60.
10. Cranston and Williams, p. 224.

Chapter 6

1. Agee and Cayce, pp. 7–8.

Chapter 8

1. Meredith Lady Young, p. 147.
2. Herbert B. Puryear, *Edgar Cayce Primer* (New York: Bantam Books, 1982), p. 69.

Chapter 9

1. Those who are seriously committed to developing their intuitive faculties and want an extensive exploration of the subject should consult Philip Goldberg's *The Intuitive Edge* (Los Angeles: Tarcher, 1983) and Frances Vaughan's *Awakening Intuition* (Garden City, N.Y.: Doubleday, 1979).
2. Stephen LaBerge, *Lucid Dreaming* (New York: Ballantine Books, 1985), p. 12.
3. Frank J. MacHovec, *Yoga: An Introduction to Inner Tranquility* (Mount Vernon, N.Y.: The Peter Pauper Press, 1972).
4. "What Is Meditation?" p. 45.

Chapter 10

1. Jeffrey Goodman, *Psychic Archaelogy* (Berkeley: Berkeley Publishing and Putnam's, 1977), pp. 3–8.
2. Goodman, pp. 31–34.
3. Goodman, pp. 89–142.
4. Corinne McLaughlin and Gordon Davidson, *Builders of the Dawn* (Walpole, N.H.: Stillpoint, 1985), pp. 237–43.

Resources

NONFICTION

Fritjof Capra. *The Tao of Physics*. New York: Bantam Books, 1977.

Gabriel Cousens, M.D. *Spiritual Nutrition and the Rainbow Diet*. Boulder, CO: Cassandra Press, 1986.

Gayle Delaney. *Living Your Dreams*. New York: Harper & Row, 1981.

Marilyn Ferguson. *The Aquarian Conspiracy*. Los Angeles: Tarcher, 1980.

Foundation for Inner Peace. *The Course in Miracles*. Tiburon, CA: Foundation for Inner Peace, 1975.

Shakti Gawain. *Creative Visualization*. New York: Bantam Books, 1982.

Philip Goldberg. *The Intuitive Edge*. Los Angeles: Tarcher, 1983.

Keith Harary and Russell Targ. *The Mind Race*. New York: Ballantine Books, 1984.

Willis H. Harman and Howard Rheingold. *Higher Creativity*. Los Angeles: Tarcher, 1984.

Gerald Jampolsky. *Love is Letting Go of Fear*. New York: Bantam Books, 1982.

Arthur Koestler. *The Roots of Coincidence*. New York: Random House, 1972.

Jeffrey Mishlove. *PSI Development Systems*. Jefferson, NC: McFarland, 1983.

Jeffrey Mishlove. *The Roots of Consciousness*. Berkeley: Random House and The Bookworks, 1975.

Robert A. Monroe. *Journeys Out of the Body*. New York: Doubleday, 1973.

Herbert B. Puryear. *The Edgar Cayce Primer.* New York: Bantam Books, 1982.

Raphael. *The Starseed Transmissions.* Mountain View, MO: Uni Sun, 1982.

Jane Roberts. *The Nature of Personal Reality.* Englewood Cliffs, NJ: Prentice-Hall, 1974.

Jason Serinus. *Psychoimmunity and the Healing Process: A Holistic Approach to Immunity and AIDS.* Berkeley: Celestial Arts, 1986.

David Spangler. *Revelation: Birth of a New Age.* Elgin, IL: Lorian Press, 1976.

Frances Vaughan. *Awakening Intuition.* Garden City, NY: Doubleday, 1979.

John White. *The Highest State of Consciousness.* New York: Doubleday, 1972.

Ken Wilbur. *The Spectrum of Consciousness.* Wheaton, IL: Theosophical Publishing House, 1977.

Meredith Lady Young. *Agartha: A Journey to the Stars.* Walpole, NH: Stillpoint, 1984.

FICTION

Richard Bach. *Illusions.* New York: Dell Books, 1977.

Dorothy Bryant. *The Kin of Ata Are Waiting for You.* Berkeley, New York: Moon Books and Random House, 1971.

Elisabeth Haich. *Initiation.* Palo Alto, CA: The Seed Center, 1974.

Shirley MacLaine. *Dancing in the Light.* New York: Bantam Books, 1985.

Shirley MacLaine. *Out on a Limb.* New York: Bantam Books, 1983.

PERIODICALS

APPLIED PSI (QUARTERLY NEWSLETTER)
The Center for Applied Intuition
2046 Clement Street
San Francisco, CA 94121

BRAIN/MIND BULLETIN (MONTHLY NEWSLETTER/REPORT)
Interface Press
P.O. Box 42211
Los Angeles, CA 90042

EAST-WEST: THE JOURNAL OF NATURAL HEALTH & LIVING
(MONTHLY MAGAZINE)
Kushi Foundation, Inc.
17 Station Street
P.O. Box 1200
Brookline, MA 02147

*METAPSYCHOLOGY: THE JOURNAL OF DISCARNATE INTELLI-
GENCE* (QUARTERLY MAGAZINE)
P.O. Box 3295
Charlottesville, VA 22903

NEW AGE JOURNAL (BIMONTHLY MAGAZINE)
Rising Star Associates, Ltd. Partnership
342 Western Avenue
Brighton, MA 02135

NEW REALITIES (BIMONTHLY MAGAZINE)
Heldref Publications
4000 Albemarle Street NW
Washington, DC 20016

SHAMAN'S DRUM (QUARTERLY MAGAZINE)
Cross-Cultural Shamanism Network
P.O. Box 2636
Berkeley, CA 94702